SATHER CLASSICAL LECTURES

Volume Fifty-Four

The Classical Foundations
of Modern Historiography

The Classical Foundations of Modern Historiography

Arnaldo Momigliano

With a Foreword by Riccardo Di Donato

University of California Press

BERKELEY · LOS ANGELES · OXFORD

University of California Press
Berkeley and Los Angeles, California

University of California Press, Ltd.
Oxford, England

© 1990 by
The Regents of the University of California

Library of Congress Cataloging-in-Publication Data

Momigliano, Arnaldo.
    The classical foundations of modern historiography / Arnaldo
Momigliano.
        p.   cm.—(Sather classical lectures ; v. 54)
    ISBN 0-520-06890-4 (alk. paper)
     1. Historiography—History.   I. Title.   II. Series.
D13.M638   1990
907'.209—dc20   89-20510
                                                    CIP

Printed in the United States of America
1   2   3   4   5   6   7   8   9

The paper used in this publication meets the minimum requirements
of American National Standard for Information Sciences—Perma-
nence of Paper for Printed Library Materials, ANSI Z39.48-1984. ∞ ™

Contents

Foreword

Invited to deliver the 1961–62 Sather Classical Lectures at the University of California at Berkeley, Arnaldo Momigliano chose a subject, *The Classical Foundations of Modern Historiography*, to which he had already given much thought.

In the preface to his *Secondo Contributo alla Storia degli Studi Classici* (1960) and in the introductory notes to several other studies of the same period, reference to the forthcoming lectures drew attention to results, already partially achieved, which were waiting to be presented in a suitable context. The choice of subjects of the individual lectures was to provide a framework in which the meaning of ancient historiography could be related to its main developments in modern historiography.

When this project was conceived, Momigliano was at the height of his intellectual maturity. Significantly, after the monographs of his precocious beginnings he had opted for the form of studies of limited length, of a length which would encourage discussion by an interested audience. Once delivered, such lectures took the form of articles in learned journals. This resulted in a certain dispersion of his work which the collections of the *Contributi* managed only partly to avoid. Momigliano himself expressed his concern, still in the second half of the sixties, that his chief areas of interest did not emerge clearly enough from the great diversity of his output.

The occasion of a series of lectures, dedicated to a subject in which he had the strongest interest, offered the possibility of putting together detailed analytical research in a comprehensive setting.

The Sather Lectures, which represented also the author's first sustained contact with American academic life, met with much success in Berkeley. They had been thought out at length in the previous two years, then written down with care, and in part, as was Momigliano's habit, rehearsed in a preliminary way before a variety of audiences.

After the last of the public lectures Momigliano wrote a brief preface, of which we have the manuscript, still dated in Berkeley, 30 March 1962, together with a copy typed in America:

> Six lectures are not supposed to exhaust an argument. If they were I should not have accepted to deliver them, because I know too little of the vast territory on which I chose to speak. The lectures are published as they were delivered and I shall be content if they provoke discussion and further exploration.
>
> The notes provide no more than some help to orientation. On most of the points raised in my lectures I have been reading and taking notes for more than thirty years. The selection from my bibliographical files is inevitably arbitrary and unjust, but, I hope, not foolish.
>
> What I have learned from the writings and the conversations of B. Croce, G. De Sanctis and F. Jacoby should be apparent at every page. My old friends F. Chabod, W. Maturi, C. Dionisotti, F. Venturi, G. Billanovich, Miss B. Smalley, helped me at every stage: the first two are no longer among us. I am conscious also of a great debt to E. Bickerman, H.-I. Marrou, H. Strasburger and F. W. Walbank. Last, but not least, I must mention with gratitude my friends and colleagues of University College London and of the Warburg Institute, and especially the wise and great librarian of the Warburg Institute, Dr. O. Kurz.
>
> My Californian colleagues—classicists and modernists—know how much I enjoyed their hospitality. The Berkeley Campanile will remain dear to my heart almost as my native Campanile.

The preface is followed by a page bearing the dedication "To the memory of Gaetano Salvemini, Marc Bloch, Johan Huizinga, Simon Dubnow, historians and witnesses of truth."

Contrary to his usual custom, however, Momigliano did not authorize immediate publication. His intention to compile the footnotes and a bibliography covering all the material dealt with soon proved to be difficult to realize. But, evidently, it also seemed to him that the completion of his original text required further work. He came back to it on several occasions during the last twenty-five years of his life. After his death on 1 September 1987 numerous copies of the Sather Lectures, with annotations and corrections, were found among his working papers. Just as a great writer ends up by identifying life with his story, the one which he is writing and the one of which he considers himself the protagonist, so Arnaldo Momigliano could not tear himself away from the subject which he felt to be crucial.

The lectures come out now in an edition which takes into account the history of their long composition. The reader should bear in mind that the book as we have it was conceived at the beginning of the sixties (after publication of the first two *Contributi*) and written in a first version between 1961 and 1962, subsequently becoming the object of careful meditation and of substantial rewriting almost fifteen years later, on the occasion of Momigliano's first lecture courses at the University of Chicago in 1975, with further revisions in the years that followed. For the revision and enrichment of the text the resources of rare books in the University Library and the Newberry Library of Chicago had proved very valuable, as he stated in September 1976 in an annual report to the Nuffield Foundation (which had awarded him a three-year research grant on his retirement from the chair of ancient history at University College London in 1975): access to this new material had given him a much more precise idea of what had been happening in Spain and Germany in the sixteenth century. The Nuffield grant enabled Momigliano to avail himself of research assistants from time to time. In an incomplete typescript produced by one of them, traces remain of an attempt at providing footnotes for each chapter, based on the author's subject card-index. This draft is not sufficient to permit authoritative reconstruction of all the footnotes which he had intended; and Momigliano's surviving autograph notes are far from complete. It has therefore been decided to publish the text without any notes.

The version now published represents the latest stage of the work left by the author, who in at least two cases—the chapters on national historiography (1975) and on Tacitism (1978)—substantially modified his text and enlarged it to almost twice the length of the original lectures.

Anne Marie Meyer has collated the typescripts of the various versions and checked the author's annotations. As a direct witness of the drafting of the two main versions and of the many intervening stages of additions and corrections, her role in establishing the text has been conclusive. The editing of the volume, the systematic checking of quotations and references, and preparation of the typescript for publication are effectively due to her: our collaboration in the final phase of editorial decisions has been for me a pleasure and an honour.

Normal conventions of a critical edition have been adopted in constituting the text, making minor changes only where consistency with the author's own general and particular criteria called for them, especially in quotations from English translations of ancient writers, which have as a rule been cited from editions in the Loeb Classical Library.

The decision not to provide a select bibliography at the end of each chapter was taken out of respect for the state of the text as left by the author and, in all likelihood, correctly interprets the reasons for the apparent noncompletion of the work. A selection does not make sense unless it corresponds in all regards to the intentions of the writer. The note that follows refers the reader to relevant works by Momigliano in which the bibliographical references selected by him are indicative of the course of his intellectual explorations.

We are grateful for helpful suggestions to Tim Cornell, Michael Crawford, Carlo Dionisotti, and Carlotta Dionisotti.

The initial statement in the text of Momigliano's Conclusion which he read at the end of his last lecture opens a chink, hitherto unknown, on a project which was to characterize the last third of his life. The trilogy which he was planning came to fruition, with the volume on the development of Greek biography and with *Alien Wisdom*, albeit in a less organic form than that here envisaged.

The publication of the present volume, which is the first constituent of the trilogy, helps towards a better understanding of the significance of the final meditations of the author—which were full of wisdom and passion—on the nature, the function, the limits, and the methods of historical research: this last contribution by Arnaldo Momigliano, like all which went before it, proceeds on the main road of the search for truth.

Riccardo Di Donato
University of Pisa
Department of Classical Philology
May 1989

Bibliographical Note

For general orientation the reader may be referred to the general sections of the bibliographies appended by Arnaldo Momigliano to the various editions of his books *The Development of Greek Biography* (Harvard University Press, 1971) and *Alien Wisdom: The Limits of Hellenization* (Cambridge University Press, 1975, 1978); to the general section on historical method in *Introduzione bibliografica alla storia greca fino a Socrate* (Florence, 1975); and to the bibliographies in the essays "Tradition and the Classical Historian," *History and Theory* XI, 3, 1972, pp. 279–293 (= *Quinto Contributo alla Storia degli Studi Classici e del Mondo Antico* [Rome, 1975], pp. 13–31), and, above all, "The Place of Ancient Historiography in Modern Historiography," in *Les études classiques aux XIXᵉ et XXᵉ siècles: leur place dans l'histoire des idées: Entretiens* tome XXVI (1979) (Fondation Hardt, Vandoeuvres-Genève, 1980), pp. 125–157 (= *Settimo Contributo*, 1984, pp. 13–36).

For the individual chapters cf.:

1. "Fattori orientali della storiografia ebraica post-esilica e della storiografia greca," in Atti del Convegno sul tema *La Persia ed il mondo greco-romano*, Roma, 11–14 aprile 1965 (Accademia Nazionale dei Lincei, 363, 76, 1966), pp. 137–146, and *Rivista Storica Italiana* LXXVII, 2, 1965, pp. 456–464 (= *Terzo Contributo*, 1966, pp. 807–818; also *Essays in Ancient and Modern Historiography* [Oxford and Middletown, Conn., 1977], pp. 25–35).

2. "Storiografia greca," *RSI* LXXXVII, 1, 1975, pp. 17–46 (= *Sesto Contributo*, 1980, pp. 33–67); "Greek Historiography," *History and Theory* XVII, 1, 1978, pp. 1–28; "History and Biography,"

in *The Legacy of Greece: A New Appraisal*, ed. by M. I. Finley (Clarendon Press, Oxford, 1981), pp. 155–184.

3. "Friedrich Creuzer and Greek Historiography," *Journal of the Warburg and Courtauld Institutes* IX, 1946, pp. 152–163 (= *Contributo*, 1955, pp. 233–248; also *Studies in Historiography* [London, 1969], pp. 75–90); "Ancient History and the Antiquarian," *JWCI* XIII, 1950, pp. 285–315 (= *Contributo*, pp. 67–106; *Studies*, pp. 1–39); "L'eredità della filologia antica e il metodo storico," *RSI* LXX, 3, 1958, pp. 442–458 (= *Secondo Contributo*, 1960, pp. 463–480).

4. "Linee per una valutazione di Fabio Pittore," *Rendiconti Accademia dei Lincei*, Classe di Scienze morali, storiche e filologiche, serie VIII, vol. XV, 7–12, 1960, pp. 310–320 (= *Terzo Contributo*, pp. 55–68); "Did Fabius Pictor Lie?" (review of A. Alföldi, *Early Rome and the Latins* [University of Michigan Press, 1965]), *New York Review of Books*, vol. V, no. 3, September 1965, pp. 19–22 (= *Essays*, pp. 99–105; *Sesto Contributo*, pp. 69–75).

5. Section "Tacitismo" of the entry "Tacito P. Cornelio" in the *Enciclopedia Italiana*, vol. XXXIII, Rome, 1936; "The First Political Commentary on Tacitus," *Journal of Roman Studies* XXXVII, 1947, pp. 91–101 (= *Contributo*, pp. 37–59; *Essays*, pp. 205–229); review of J. von Stackelberg, *Tacitus in der Romania: Studien zur literarischen Rezeption des Tacitus in Italien and Frankreich* (Tübingen, 1960), *Archiv für das Studium der Neueren Sprachen und Literaturen* 200, 1, 1963, p. 75 (= *Terzo Contributo*, pp. 775–776); review of R. Häussler, *Tacitus und das historische Bewusstsein* (Heidelberg, 1965), *RSI* LXXVIII, 4, 1966, pp. 974–976 (= *Quinto Contributo*, pp. 1007–1010); review of K. C. Schellhase, *Tacitus in Renaissance Political Thought* (University of Chicago Press, 1976), *Classical Philology* 47, 1, 1979, pp. 72–74 (= *Settimo Contributo*, pp. 499–502).

6. "L'età del trapasso fra storiografia antica e storiografia medievale," *RSI* LXXXI, 2, 1969, pp. 286–303 (= *Quinto Contributo*, pp. 49–71); "Popular Religious Beliefs and the Late Roman Historians," in *Studies in Church History*, vol. 8, eds. Canon G. J. Cuming and Derek Baker (Cambridge University Press, 1971), pp. 1–18 (= *Quinto Contributo*, pp. 73–92; *Essays*, pp. 141–159); "Historiography of Religion: The Western Tradition," in *The Encyclopedia of Religon*, vol. 6 (New York, 1987), pp. 383–390 (= *Ottavo Contributo*, 1987, pp. 27–44).

Introduction

The growth of social history and archaeology is the clearest sign that something has been happening in the kingdom of Clio since the days of Thucydides. In the nineteenth century three historians as different as Ranke, Macaulay, and Eduard Meyer regarded Thucydides as the model historian. This opinion still finds supporters. One of them, the late Professor Gomme, was one of my predecessors in the Sather chair a few years ago. But even Gomme's wonderful pugnacity was no longer sufficient to persuade many of us that Thucydides cannot be improved upon. Thucydides wrote as a student of contemporary political and military history. The method he developed was that of a political and military historian of his own times. The historians of the twentieth century can explore any period of the past as if it were contemporary history in the Thucydidean sense because they know how to exploit types of evidence that take us back to almost any past. Furthermore, the very notion of political history nowadays raises so many issues in relation to other aspects of history that it has ceased to indicate something definite and recognisable. Books like Huizinga's *Waning of the Middle Ages*, or Marc Bloch's *Caractères originaux de l'histoire rurale française*, or even Perry Miller's *The New England Mind* cannot be presented as mere developments of the Thucydidean type of history. While these books also have their antecedents in Antiquity, we must look for such in the field of antiquarian and erudite research rather than in the tradition of Thucydidean history. The variety and complexity of our present work in history give new prominence to links with the classical world which were previously neglected.

If ancient erudite research is the obvious antecedent of so much of our cultural and social history, our interest in ecclesiastical history represents a link with ancient ecclesiastical historiography. Our study of conscious, subconscious, and unconscious historical motivation gives a new value to the psychological history of Tacitus and calls attention to his enormous authority among students of history and politics from the early sixteenth to the early nineteenth century. The fact that mere political historiography is now discredited and generally recognised to be tedious invites a reassessment of our debt to Greek historians. At the same time, we have come to realise that Greek historiography was not naturally and inevitably destined to become the foundation of our Western historiography. We should not have inherited Greek historiography without the bold intervention of some Romans who made Greek historiography the historiography of the Roman Empire. Above all we should not have our national histories without the example of Roman national historiography, and more specifically without the example of Livy. Even so Greek historiography had to compete with Hebrew historiography. Both Greek and postexilic Hebrew historiography came into existence against the background of the Persian Empire and clearly show their common origin. Later Jewish and Greek historians competed with each other, and it is a matter of research to determine how much of Jewish thought passed into Christian works such as the ecclesiastical histories of Late Antiquity.

If these preliminary considerations are valid there is some justification for asking the following six questions: (1) What have Greek and Jewish historiographies in common and why and to what extent did Greek historiography ultimately prevail? (2) Why did Thucydides rather than Herodotus become the most authoritative historian of Antiquity? (3) What part did the antiquarians play in historical research? (4) How was Greek historiography imported into Rome and what did the romanisation of Greek historiography entail? (5) What is the place of Tacitus in historical thought? (6) Why and in what way has ecclesiastical historiography a tradition of its own?

To each of these questions I have devoted one of the six lectures which I have the great honour to deliver in this University. I have intentionally left aside other questions that are related to my subject. I shall not discuss the biographical tradition and shall not try to assess the influence of ancient theories of history on later philosophy and methodology of history. I could adduce various reasons for my silence on these matters (one is my suspicion that out of a hundred persons who can explain an event only one or two have the technical ability—the historian's equipment—to decide whether that event was an event at all—whether it happened). But it is more honest to admit that at the moment I do not know enough about the history of biography and about the history of the philosophy of history to attempt even the most superficial generalisations about them. I hope to be able later on to do some specific work on the history of biography. I do not feel, however, that my present argument is seriously affected by the absence of a discussion of biography and of theories of history. I am more concerned about the enormous gaps in my knowledge of the subjects on which I have chosen to speak. I shall try not to conceal the lacunae of which I am aware; and I should like to ask my audience to accept what I shall say as a provisional attempt to reassess the value of ancient historiography in the light of the twentieth-century revolution in history writing.

CHAPTER ONE

Persian Historiography, Greek Historiography, and Jewish Historiography

I

We are increasingly aware of the fact that both Greeks and Jews developed some of the most characteristic features of their civilizations within the frame of the Persian Empire. It therefore makes sense to ask whether both Greek historiography and Jewish postexilic historiography were influenced either by Persian historiography or by other literary traditions to be found in the Persian Empire. But this question is only one of the several questions we can ask in comparing Jewish and Greek historiography. We can for instance ask: (1) What have Greek and biblical historiography in common? (2) Which, on the other hand, are the main differences between Greek and biblical historiography? (3) Why did Greek historiography prove to be so vital while Jewish historiography ended, rather abruptly, in the first century A.D.?

My lecture is consequently divided into six parts: (1) on Persian historiography; (2) on the general acquaintance of Greek and Jewish historians with Persian affairs; (3) on specific points of possible Oriental influence on Greek and Jewish historians; (4) on certain features of the reaction of the Greek and Jewish historians to the political situation represented by the Persian Empire; (5) on the most characteristic differences between Greek and Jewish historians; and (6) on the reasons why Jewish historiography died out prematurely.

II

In the perfectly respectable circles in which I moved when I was young, it was a dogma that if you wanted to study Persian history you had to know Greek, but if you wanted to learn Greek history you had to know German. Herodotus was the authority for Persian history, Karl Julius Beloch for Greek history.

The situation may have changed in Greek history. But Persian history is still in the hands of Herodotus. The decipherment of the Behistun inscription and the excavations of Persepolis and Susa, however far-reaching, have not done for Persia what the same kind of work has done for Egypt and Babylonia. If the progress in Oriental history can be measured in terms of emancipation from Herodotus, it is evident that Persian history has not been revolutionised by modern methods of research as much as Mesopotamian and Egyptian history has been. In the early years of this century Eduard Meyer was commissioned to write the article "Persia in Antiquity" for the eleventh edition of the *Encyclopaedia Britannica*. The article appeared in 1911 and is still fresh. No article on Egypt, Mesopotamia, or Asia Minor in Antiquity could have survived so long.

The fact that we get most of our information about the ancient Persians from Greek sources does not mean that the Persians relied on the alien races of their empire for the preservation of the record of their own activities. They had their own historiography either in Persian or in Aramaic. We all know what a Persian king did when he suffered from insomnia: "On that night could not the king sleep, and he commanded to bring the book of records of the chronicles; and they were read before the king" (6, 1). The Book of Esther can be trusted in the matter of chronicles, if not of the insomnia. The Book of Esther may also imply that the Persian chronicles contained documents: "And all the acts of his [Ahasuerus'] power and of his might, and the full account of the greatness of Mordecai, how the king advanced him, are they not written in the book of the chronicles of the kings of Media and Persia?" (10, 2). But this implication is by no means certain. The Books of Ezra and Nehemiah, whose knowledge of Persian institutions is beyond dispute, confirm the existence of Persian Royal Chronicles. In one of the Aramaic documents relating to the opposition against the rebuilding of the walls of Jerusalem, King Artaxerxes I is asked to read the chronicles of his ancestors, where he will find evidence about the past rebellions of Jerusalem (Ezra 4, 15). The writer obviously presupposes that the kings of Persia had access to chronicles on events of pre-Persian times. He was certainly correct. Babylonian chronicles, if nothing else, were available for consultation about the more remote past. Also the Greek Ctesias claimed to have used the royal records "in which the Persians in accordance with a certain law of theirs kept an account of their ancient affairs" (Diod. II, 33, 4).

But the Persian chronicles disappeared very early. As far as we know, the Chronicles of the Sassanian Kings, which the Byzantine Agathias mentions in the sixth century A.D., were not in any way connected with the Chronicles of the Achaemenid Kings. As Th. Nöldeke observed long ago, one of the striking features about the Persian revival under the Sassanian kings is that they knew almost nothing about the Achaemenids. The historical and political tradition of the Achaemenids had gone overboard long before the revolution of the third century A.D. which purported to restore Persian national values. The Avesta does not mention either Darius or Xerxes. When Firdausi came to write the *Shanameh* in the tenth century, the break with the Achaemenid past had been almost complete for more than a thousand years.

Inscriptions are the only surviving evidence for the way in which the Persians thought about history. They are of limited value for obvious reasons. Nobody would describe the *Res Gestae Divi Augusti* as Augustus' autobiography. In fact we know that the Roman emperor did write his autobiography in a very different form. There is no reason to apply another criterion to that remote ancestor of the *Res Gestae*, namely, the account King Darius gave of himself in the Behistun or Bisutun inscription. His purpose was self-glorification in a limited number of words, not a complete autobiography. In the case of the Behistun inscription there is the additional difficulty that we do not know whether King Darius wrote it for men or for gods to read. By putting his inscription on a rock 300 feet high over the road, and by barring the access to it, he made his words available only to professional rock climbers or to gods. He certainly wrote for select circles. But copies of the inscription circulated later, and one wonders whether this circulation was centrally organised. With all this the Behistun inscription teaches us something about the Persian attitude to history. First of all, it shows that the Persians were capable of some kind of autobiography written in the first person. Second, the account is basically factual, clear and free from any miraculous intervention. When the Behistun inscription was deciphered, scholars were surprised to see that it confirmed Herodotus in so many precise details, such as the names of the rebellious Magi. Perhaps it would have been more appropriate to be surprised that the Persian inscription proved to be on an equal historical level with Herodotus. The King of Persia relies on his own gods, but direct intervention of gods in miraculous forms is not mentioned. The outlook is aristocratic, not theological. The pride of the Achaemenids in their ancestry is notorious. Darius emphasises his physical and moral superiority: his enemies are the lie, he is the truth. The loyalty of the satraps is his main concern. He relishes cruelty against conquered rebels. But other inscriptions show that his attitude towards subjects and external enemies was not always so barbaric. We could get something for our purpose from the final section of the Babylonian chronicle of Nabonidus, which records the triumph of Cyrus over his enemy, if we were certain that this part of the chronicle was directly inspired by Cyrus or his staff. There are curious touches of irony in this final section from which we may well suspect that a Persian must have had a hand in describing the ineptitude of the last Babylonian king. But the matter is too uncertain, and the chronicle of Nabonidus as a whole belongs to another tradition.

What we clearly perceive in the Persian historical inscriptions is a king-centered society, a strongly aristocratic outlook, an emphasis on loyalty accompanied by corresponding violence of intrigues and passions. On the other hand we have seen that to a Persian the facts were facts. Old Persian with its easy syntactical structure and its clear verbal system was not a bad instrument for historical prose. If we discount the monotony of the formulas and the narrowness of the subject matter, we can see that here there is a historical style in the making.

III

So much for the direct evidence on Old Persian historiography. Our next question is whether Persian historiography, such as we can dimly perceive it through direct or indirect evidence, influenced the devel-

opment of Greek historiography on the one side and of Hebrew historiography on the other. We have no evidence that the Jews knew
Greek historians or that the Greeks knew Jewish historians before the
third century B.C., but there is indisputable evidence that the Greek
and Jewish historians were in contact with the Persians. I am well
aware that Photius in his summary of Diodorus' Book XL attributes to
Hecataeus of Miletus a description of Jewish religion which, if authentic, would imply that Hecataeus of Miletus knew something about the
Sacred Books of the Jews at the end of the sixth century B.C. Nor am
I unaware that Franz Dornseiff, a scholar for whom I have the greatest
respect, has definitely maintained that the fragment is authentic and
implies the direct acquaintance of Hecataeus of Miletus with Jewish
religion. But I am quite certain that either Photius or Diodorus attributed the fragment on the Jews to the wrong Hecataeus. The Hecataeus
who spoke about the Jews was not the man of Miletus who lived before the Persian Wars, but his namesake of Abdera who wrote in the
fourth century B.C.—a well-known authority on the Jews.

The evidence for contacts between Greek historians and the Persian
world is easy to summarise. The rise of Greek historiography is closely
connected with that of geographical studies. The first Greek to write
about his geographical explorations—Scylax of Caryanda, a traveller
in the Persian Gulf and elsewhere—did so in the pay and by the order
of King Darius in about 500 B.C. (Herod. IV, 44). Hecataeus of Miletus, a geographer and genealogist, wrote under the Persians. He was
interested in Oriental genealogies and compared Greek with non-
Greek evidence. He travelled in the Persian Empire as a Persian subject
in its heyday. His successor Herodotus was born a Persian subject in
the Greek city of Halicarnassus. He never liked the Ionian rebellion,
though he was fully aware of the meaning of the Greek victory over the
Persian Empire. He travelled in countries which were or had been Persian. Though he never saw Persia itself and was unable to speak any
foreign language, his histories are teeming with alleged Persian traditions. They came to him secondhand and clearly distorted. But we
must never lose sight of the primary fact that the discovery of the Behistun inscription confirmed Herodotus' position as our most reliable
witness for Persian affairs. Even in Athens, Herodotus was able to find

an aristocratic Persian refugee, Zopyrus son of Megabyzus, and to talk
to him in Greek about Persia (III, 160). We should like to know more
about Xanthus the Lydian, a contemporary of Herodotus, who wrote
in Greek as a Persian subject about the history of his own country, Ly-
dia. The same applies to other fifth-century writers, such as Dionysius
of Miletus, Hellanicus of Mytelene, and Charon of Lampsacus, who
collected Persian traditions in places where acquaintance with Persian
customs and peoples must have been fairly easy and common. They at
least prove the constant concern of early Greek historians with Persian
history—not a reason for surprise. In the next generation Ctesias of
Cnidus is our big disappointment. He was a doctor to Artaxerxes
Mnemon before 405 B.C. and claimed to have lived at the Persian court
for seventeen years. He certainly knew Persian, and, if he had wanted
to, he could have collected an immense amount of direct information
about Persian history. Unfortunately he seems to have been more concerned with sensationalism than with truth, and was obsessed by the
preoccupation of giving Herodotus the lie. The result, as F. Jacoby has
seen, is that Ctesias is more of a novelist than a historian. Yet he is not
useless to us. The fact that he was a liar does not mean that he had not
absorbed the atmosphere of the Oriental court with its love intrigues
and unreliable tales. We are entitled to ask the question whether his
fantastic tales are infected by Persian habits of storytelling. The list of
persons who travelled in Persian territory and wrote about Persian history goes on throughout the fourth century. Xenophon is another obvious name, though in the *Cyropaedia* he clearly did not intend to
write history: the *Cyropaedia* is a well-defined philosophic utopia of a
type known also from other Socratics. What I have said is enough to
remind us that Greek historiography in its early stages was concerned
with Persia and was practised by men whose acquaintance with Persian traditions is beyond dispute.

As for the Jews, the evidence of the Persian impact is clear enough
in general. If H. Schaeder was right, Ezra's title as "scribe of the law of
the God of heaven" means that he was a Persian official in charge of
Jewish affairs. If Schaeder was wrong, the activity of the mysterious
Ezra still remains to be explained in a Persian context: he cannot be
wiped out of history. The more open Nehemiah tells us that he was the

cupbearer of Artaxerxes I. The autobiographies of both Ezra and Nehemiah, which are incorporated in the books that bear their names, provide the confirmation of their acquaintance with Persian ways. The Books of Daniel, Judith, and Esther are a more difficult matter. Each of the three books preserves features of the Achaemenid period and raises the problem of whether the story it tells originated before Alexander the Great. The Book of Daniel has some authentic details about the fall of Babylon, such as Belshazzar's banquet and the very name of Belshazzar, though Daniel mistakenly takes him to be the son of Nebuchadnezzar, not the son and co-ruler of Nabonidus. The story of Esther is enacted entirely at the Persian court. The story is absurd, but many details about the Persian court ring true. For instance, the author knows about the seven privileged men who "saw the king's face and sat first in the kingdom" (1, 14), and has a clear idea of the Persian postal service (8, 10). The story of Judith has Holofernes as the chief villain and the eunuch Bagoas as his adjutant. The two names are common enough, but they appear together only in the expedition of Artaxerxes III Ochos against Phoenicia and Egypt about 350 B.C. The coincidence can hardly be fortuitous. On the other hand, as we all know, the authors of these three books vie with each other in historical incompetence. It would take too long to tell of the mistakes of Daniel. It will be enough to remind ourselves that according to Daniel, Darius the Mede—a non-existent monster—not Cyrus the Persian, conquered Babylon and that the kings of Persia from Cyrus to Alexander were four, not eleven. As to the Book of Esther, Mordecai was deported to Babylon in 597 but was appointed grand vizier in the twelfth year of King Xerxes, that is, 124 years later, in 473 B.C. His cousin Esther was presumably a hundred years younger than he. According to the Book of Judith the Jews returned from exile and rededicated the temple under Nebuchadnezzar, who is described as reigning "over the Assyrians at Nineveh." At the end of the seventeenth century the great Montfaucon, mastering all the resources of the learning of his time, was unable to make sense of this howler. His failure was one of the first signs that the citadel of traditional biblical exegesis was beginning to crumble under the attacks of critics such as Hugo Grotius.

The late date of the three books, while it explains their mistakes, is not of course incompatible with the preservation of genuine Persian elements. Indeed we have to reckon with the possibility of some of the contents of the three books going back to non-Jewish sources. There is something to be said for the theory that the Book of Esther goes back to a non-Jewish model. The festival of Purim, which the Book of Esther purports to explain, was non-Jewish in origin, as its non-Hebrew name shows. Daniel has no obvious antecedent in extant Jewish literature, and is hardly to be separated from non-Jewish texts such as the Demotic Chronicle. Details are obscure and controversial, but we must never forget that the Jews of the postexilic period spoke Aramaic and therefore were able to read the gentile literature in this international language of the Persian Empire. There is of course a difference between the position of the Jews and the position of the Ionian Greeks in the Persian Empire. The Persian rule over the Jews was continuous for two centuries. The Persian rule over the Ionian Greeks was interrupted by Athenian control for the greater part of the fifth century. Our question is, however, the same in both cases: how much did the ruler influence the historiography of the ruled?

There are three ways in which this influence could manifest itself. One is the direct influence of Persian historiography. The second is the influence of other Oriental historiographies accessible within the Persian Empire. The third is the more generic influence of Oriental institutions and literary traditions other than historiography. I shall suggest that the influence of Oriental institutions and literary traditions other than historiography appears to have been the most important. But first we must examine the evidence.

IV

I want to examine the evidence under three heads: (1) the use of documents in historiography; (2) the autobiographical and biographical tradition; and (3) the novelistic background.

I begin with the documents. On the Jewish side the question is simpler. Jewish postexilic historiography is characterised by extensive verbatim quotation of documents which come or are alleged to come from archives. This is different from the implicit utilisation of official documents, such as the list of Solomon's highest officials, which is to be found in the Books of Kings (I, 4), or from the quotation of poetry, such as Deborah's song (Judges 5). The authenticity of the documents does not concern us here, though I would call authentic the majority of the documents given in Ezra and Nehemiah, in the Books of Maccabees, and in Josephus, who inherited the habit of quoting documents from his Jewish predecessors. Ezra is aware of the importance the Persians attached to documents in order to establish legal rights, and so is the Book of Esther (9, 32). It seems natural to relate this feature of Jewish postexilic historiography to the impact of Persian example—either in administrative practice or perhaps (though this is very uncertain) in the historiographical practice of the Royal Chronicles.

The Greek side of the matter is far less clear. The Greeks wrote history as free people. They were not so obsessed by the need to claim rights from their overlords as the Jews were under the Persians, the Seleucids, and the Romans. This is enough to explain why Greek historiography is much less concerned with the literal quotation of documents. Herodotus quotes only inscriptions, oracles, and other poems. He uses, however, other written documents, such as the list of the satrapies (III, 89), the description of the Persian postal service (V, 52), and the catalogue of the Persian army (VII, 61). Each of these texts presents a problem with regard to its origins and its value. But it is difficult to reject out of hand the first impression that there is some Persian document behind each of them. Herodotus seems to be acquainted with Persian documentary evidence.

Among the Greek historians we possess, Thucydides is the first to copy documents ultimately coming from archives. Curiously enough, several of these documents concern Persia. Out of eleven documents quoted verbatim by Thucydides, five have to do with Persia: the two letters exchanged between Pausanias and Xerxes and the three versions of the Persian-Spartan agreement of 411 B.C. Wilamowitz and E. Schwartz thought that if Thucydides had finished his work he would have eliminated the documents, as they run contrary to his style. Nobody can say what Thucydides would have done if he had finished his work, but it is true that there is something surprising in the inclusion of these documents. Why did Thucydides choose to introduce them?

Was he preceded by some Ionian historian who was nearer to Oriental habits? We cannot say. The only footnote I want to add is that our next reference to a document in Greek historiography is apparently the letter of the Persian or Median king Stronaggaius to Queen Zaraenaia in a fragment of Ctesias discovered not very long ago (Pap. Ox. 2330 = fr. 8b Jacoby). This is a forgery by Ctesias himself, and a ridiculous one at that. But we are again on Persian territory. Hellanicus (fr. 178 Jacoby) knew that Persian kings communicated by letter.

I pass to the second point on autobiographical and biographical style. As is well known, the Chronicler who put together the Books of Ezra and Nehemiah in their present form used parts of their autobiographies. Nehemiah's autobiography is splendidly preserved. Ezra's memoirs are sadly mutilated, and may not even be authentic. The chronological order of some sections has clearly been upset: a pity, because one would give something to know more about this lonely and almost inhumanly harsh fighter for the Torah. It is now generally recognised that the two autobiographical fragments cannot be treated in isolation from the vast Oriental tradition of autobiographical writing in the first person. Professor Mowinckel was inclined to connect at least Nehemiah's autobiography with the Babylonian documents of this kind rather than with the Persian ones. This is a question more of taste than of argument. Other scholars have shown parallels in Egyptian autobiographies. The Behistun inscription of Darius was known in its Aramaic version to the Jews of Elephantina more or less at the time when Ezra and Nehemiah wrote. Both Ezra and Nehemiah gave a Jewish twist to the general Oriental—and also specifically Persian—tradition of autobiography in the first person.

What about the Greeks? There was always a tradition of autobiographical accounts in Greek literature. Nestor telling of his youth is almost a conscious joke in the Iliad, and Odysseus never spared details about himself, whether authentic or not. Hesiod tells us about himself and his father and brother. Lyrics and tragedy are full of accounts in the first person. Heraclitus and Empedocles have superb passages about themselves in the first person. On the other hand lengthy autobiographical prose in the first person is a rare event in classical Greece. The most obvious case in the fifth century B.C. is that of Ion of Chios, who wrote in the first person about people he knew. He tells how he met Sophocles at a banquet in 440 B.C. Hecataeus of Miletus started his historical book with a programmatic declaration in the first person. Both Hecataeus and Ion of Chios belonged to Ionian culture, where Oriental influences were active.

Another observation is perhaps more important. Scylax wrote a biography of Heraclides, the tyrant of Mylasa. Both the writer and his subject lived in the Persian sphere. In Herodotus the best personal stories (for instance, the biography of Democedes) come from the Eastern side. Metropolitan Greece provided very little biographical material for Herodotus. Even Thucydides pays attention to biographical details only when his heroes—Pausanias and Themistocles—are to be found on the fringes of the Persian Empire. We may suspect that the Greeks of Asia Minor were more interested in biographical details than the Greeks, say, of Sparta or Athens.

These considerations lead us to our third point, on the novelistic background of Jewish and Greek historiography. In the international society of the Persian Empire people told stories on an international scale. The classic case of a pagan story turned into a Jewish one is the story of Achikar, which was known to the Jews of Elephantina as early as the fifth century B.C. and reappears in the Book of Tobit. The Greeks certainly knew the Achikar story in the fourth century B.C., and Democritus may have been acquainted with it in the late fifth century. Take another novelistic motif. According to Herodotus, Otanes managed to find out that the alleged Smerdis son of Cyrus was a fraud. Otanes' daughter Phaedima was in the harem of Pseudo-Smerdis, and her father encouraged her to discover the truth. The words of Otanes—"Daughter, thou art of noble blood"—and the answer of Phaedima—"It will be a great risk, nevertheless I will venture"—might be part of a communication between Mordecai and Esther. In the Book of Judith, Holofernes enquires about the Jews in a way which is very similar to Atossa's questions about the Athenians in Aeschylus' *Persae* (230–265). The Herodotean story of Intaphernes' wife, who prefers saving her brother to saving husband and children (III, 119), is genuinely Oriental, as Nöldeke showed long ago. When Wilamowitz remarked that Judith could find a place in Parthenius' stories, he was

purposely one-sided. No Greek heroine could be so pedantically orthodox as Judith. But Wilamowitz recognised by implication that the
novelistic background was international.

V

We have now reached some positive and some negative results.
There are clearly Oriental elements both in Jewish and in Greek historiography, but these are to be attributed to the common cultural
background of the Persian Empire rather than to specific Persian influence. If there is specific Persian influence, it is limited to the use of documents—and perhaps to the autobiographical style.

These elements of direct Oriental influence are interesting enough in
themselves, but they are partly conjectural and were in any case never
decisive for the future of Greek and Jewish historiography. What is decisive is the common reaction of Greeks and Jews to the royal chronicles of the Eastern Empires.

In pre-exilic times the Jews had had chronicles of their kings. The
author or authors of the present Books of Kings used them. But the
Books of Kings we read now are not comparable with the ordinary
Royal Chronicles we know from Assyria and must assume to have existed in Persia. The Books of Kings are a record of events connected
with the relationship between Jehovah and the Hebrew nation as a
whole. This of course applies even more to the definite postexilic products which we call the Books of Ezra and Nehemiah and Chronicles.
These are histories of a religious society. Two or three centuries later
the author of the First Book of Maccabees showed that this tradition
of the political and religious historian was still alive among the Jews.

In Greece chronicles played a modest part, if any, in the origins of
Greek historiography. Books on individual nations and accounts of big
wars almost certainly preceded local history. Thanks to Herodotus and
Thucydides the Greeks acquired what was going to remain their characteristic historiography, the history of one big historical event or of
one or more cities in their internal upheavals and external warfare.

Starting from very different presuppositions, Greeks and Jews both developed a kind of history which was not a chronicle of individual kings or heroes, but a chronicle of a political community. Both the Jewish and the Greek type of political history broke with the Persian or more generally Oriental type of history centred on the performances of individual kings or heroes: it expressed the life of societies deliberating and acting with clear purposes under the leadership of far-seeing men.

In the last resort the similarity between the Jewish and the Greek types of political history appears to be due not to the influence of Persia, but to reaction against Persia. This is no reason for surprise. In the sixth, fifth, and fourth centuries B.C. both the Greeks and the Jews reorganised their communal life in conscious reaction to the surrounding civilisation which was the Persian Empire. It is a great compliment to Persia that both did so without hating her. Indeed the Persians helped the Jews to establish their theocracy. In the same way they were ready to replace tyranny by democracy in Greek cities when they felt that democracy was wanted. Deutero-Isaiah among the Jews and Aeschylus among the Greeks recognised the ethical qualities of the Persian ruling class and made it a starting point for their religious meditation. The reshaping of political life in Greece after the Persian Wars occasionally took a turn that reminds us of parallel events in Judaea. The building of the wall of the Piraeus was no less important and no less opposed by external rivals than the rebuilding of the wall of Jerusalem. The elimination of mixed marriages in Judaea reminds us of the decree of 451–450 which deprived of Athenian citizenship those unable to prove their dual Athenian parentage. Both in Judaea and in Greece an internationally minded society was being replaced by a narrower and consequently more communally minded society. Men who, like Ezra and Nehemiah, Miltiades and Themistocles, had had close contact with Persia were replaced by leaders more rooted in the local tradition. Jewish and Greek historiography expressed the outlook of groups emerging to new life away from the influence of Persia, but not without having experienced the ethical and religious quality of the Persian rulers, and not without having learned something of their technique in recording events.

VI

The next question is: What were the main differences between Hebrew and Greek historians?

Each Greek historian is of course different from the others, but all Greek historians deal with a limited subject which they consider important, and all are concerned with the reliability of the evidence they are going to use. Greek historians never claim to tell all the facts of history from the origins of the world, and never believe that they can tell their tale without *historia*, without research. Each Greek historian is concerned with the qualitative importance of what he is going to say. His task is to preserve the memory of important past events and to present the facts in a trustworthy and attractive way. The choice of the subject and the examination of the evidence depend on various factors—including the intellectual integrity of the historian himself. Ctesias, who claimed to be a careful researcher, turns out to be a liar. The point, however, is that he had to claim to be a trustworthy researcher in order to be respectable. There is an important implication in all this. The Greek historian almost invariably thinks that the past events he tells have some relevance to the future. The events would not be important if they did not teach something to those who read about them. The story will provide an example, constitute a warning, point to a likely pattern of future developments in human affairs. There is no indication in Greek historians that events inevitably recur at stated intervals. The often-repeated notion that the Greek historians had a cyclical idea of time is a modern invention. There is only one Greek historian, namely Polybius, who applies the notion of cycle to historical events, but he does it only partially with regard to the evolution of constitutions—and leaves ordinary military and political events out of the cycle. Even in the case of constitutions his theory has nothing of the rigour and coherence attributed to it by some modern interpreters. What the Greek attitude to history almost invariably implied was that the historian not only tells the facts, but tries to establish a connection between them: in other words he looks for causes and consequences, and may be rather sophisticated at that. In order to have the correct sequence, without which no reliable explanation is possible, events must be dated. Since its early stages Greek historiography was concerned with chronology, though it would be wrong to assert that chronological research among the Greeks served only the purpose of causal explanation. Chronology was necessary also because antiquity or long duration or both were criteria of importance. Thucydides was an exception in admiring the Constitution of the Five Thousand, which was both recent and short-lived (VIII, 97). The ordinary Greek liked what lasted long or at least what was very ancient.

On the other hand the Greek historians were very conscious of the importance of literary presentation. At least from Thucydides' time onwards they knew that under certain circumstances an attractive literary form might become contrary to the interests of truth. More generally the Greek historian was always aware of being in danger of saying something that was not true or even probable. Not that he invariably cared to avoid the danger. But the choice between what is true and what is untrue, or at least between what is probable and what is improbable, was inherent in the profession of the historian as the Greeks understood it.

If we pass to the Hebrew historians, as we read them in the Bible, the picture is different. Once upon a time the Hebrew historians selected special periods for their books: we know of a chronicle of Solomon's reign (I Kings 11, 41), but what we have in the Bible is a continuous story from the beginning of the world. If we follow the theory that the so-called Yahwist compiled the first draft of such a continuous history, we must go back for it to the tenth or ninth century B.C. This is not to say that the men who put together the historical books of the Bible, as we have them, had no principle of selection. The selection was that of a privileged line of events which showed Jehovah's special relation with Israel. Thus to the Hebrew historian historiography soon became a narration of events from the beginning of the world such as no Greek historian ever conceived. The criteria of reliability were also different. Jews have always been supremely concerned with truth. The Hebrew God is the God of Truth. No Greek god, to the best of my knowledge, is called ἀληθινός, truthful. If God is Truth, his followers have the duty to preserve a truthful record of the events in which God showed his presence. Each generation is obliged to transmit a true account of what happened to the next generation. Remembrance of the past is a religious duty for the Jews which was unknown to the Greeks. Consequently reliability in Jewish terms coincides with the truthfulness of the transmitters and with the ultimate truth of God in whom the transmitters believe. Such reliability was supposed to be further supported by written records to an extent which was unknown to Greek cities. Flavius Josephus boasted—not unreasonably—that the Jews had better-organised public records than the Greeks (*c. Apionem*, I, 1ff.).

What Josephus seems to have missed is that the Greeks had criteria by which to judge the relative merits of various versions which the Jewish historians had not. The very existence of different versions of the same event is something which, as far as I remember, is not noticed as such by the biblical historians. The distinction between various versions in the Bible is a modern application of Greek methods to biblical studies. In Hebrew historiography the collective memory about past events could never be verified according to objective criteria. If priests forged records—and priests are notoriously inclined to pious frauds in all centuries—the Hebrew historian did not possess the critical instrument to discover the forgery. In so far as modern historiography is a critical one, it is a Greek, not a Jewish, product.

This, however, does not end the story. The Greeks liked history, but never made it the foundation of their lives. The educated Greek turned to rhetorical schools, to mystery cults, or to philosophy for guidance. History was never an essential part of the life of a Greek—not even (one suspects) for those who wrote it. There may be many reasons for this attitude of the Greeks, but surely an important factor was that history was so open to uncertainties, so unlikely to provide undisputed guidance. To the biblical Hebrew, history and religion were one. This identification, via the Gospels, has never ceased to be relevant to Christian civilisation. Yet we know the paradox inherent in this situation. The Greeks never lost interest in history and transmitted this interest as part of their cultural inheritance. The Jews, to whom history meant so much more, abandoned the practice of historiography almost entirely from the second to the sixteenth century and returned to historical study only under the impact of the Italian Renaissance.

The question of how Greek historiography survived its Christianisation will have to be faced in other contexts. It will be enough to suggest here that Greek historiography survived because a distinction was introduced between sacred and profane history. But we want to ask as our last question: What then stopped Hebrew historiography from developing any further and competing with Greek historiography?

VII

We must beware of ready-made answers. In more than one sense there was no lack of research among Jewish historians. If by research we mean discovery of documents in archives or utilisation of earlier histories, we have seen that there was plenty of it. On the other hand if by research we mean care in depicting a contemporary political situation, the Books of Ezra and Nehemiah and the First Book of Maccabees are fine specimens. They give us a coherent picture of a political development, and they allow us to see what actually happened. They are more than material for future historians. They are thought-out historiography. There was nothing wrong with this Jewish historiography except, quite simply, that it died out and did not become part of the Jewish way of life. The Jews did not go on writing history. They lost interest in historical research. Even the First Book of Maccabees ceased to be a Jewish book. Its original Hebrew text was allowed to fade out, and the Greek translation was preserved by the Christians. The appearance of the Book of Daniel in the Jewish canon would call for many a comment. But one is enough for my purpose. Fantastic speculations about historical developments are not necessarily contrary to the interest of historical studies. They offer a scheme for the coordination of historical events. They are a constant challenge to the learned who pile up the facts without being able to organise them. Even today there are professors of history who would get inspiration from a careful reading of Daniel. But any principle of coordination of the facts is useful only if the facts are available. Where history is studied, even Daniel is useful. The facts were available to the Christians. It is unnecessary to explain here what an important part the Book of Daniel played in Christian philosophy of history from Clement of Alexandria to Hegel. The uselessness or near uselessness of Daniel in the Jewish tradition is due to the absence of historical research among the Jews.

Our question, therefore, can be reformulated in a slightly different form: Why did the Jews lose interest in historical research? The reality of this change cannot be doubted. The very way in which history is treated in the Books of Daniel, Esther, Judith, and, one could add, Tobit, shows that by the second century B.C. the interest in history was at a very low level. The First Book of Maccabees, which was written about 100 B.C., was probably already an exceptional production. Some historical books were certainly written in Hebrew or Aramaic even later. Flavius Josephus wrote one in Aramaic before turning into a Greek historian. But the gap between the disappearance of the Aramaic Josephus and the appearance of the so-called Josippon in Italy in the tenth century is enormous. Indeed the gap extends further because it was not until the sixteenth century that Italian Jews began to display a serious interest in Jewish history. Nothing can fill the gap—neither the minute compilation of the *Megillath Ta'anit* nor the *Seder 'Olam Rabbah*, nor indeed the so-called *Liber antiquitatum biblicarum*, which was written in Hebrew, perhaps in the first century A.D., but is now only preserved in a later translation for Christian use. Other writings, such as the *Megillath Antiochos*, which is without any historical value, do not even deserve to be taken into consideration in this context. The only type of historical tradition in which the Jews really remained interested (apart from biblical events) was the relation of the various rabbis to their predecessors: the *Seder Tannaim Wa-Amoraim* is a late (ninth century), but fairly typical, example of what we could call history of the transmission of learning. It was observed by Moritz Steinschneider that the medieval Jews took an interest in all aspects of Arabic culture—mathematics, philosophy, medicine, poetry—except history. Steinschneider quotes an eloquent passage by Maimonides, who declares historical books to be a mere waste of time.

The disappearance of the Jewish state is no sufficient explanation of the end of Jewish historiography, though it was certainly a contributory cause. Jewish historiography was in a critical condition even before the end of the Jewish state, and there is no law of nature by which historiography should end when political independence ends. The

Greeks did not lose interest in history when they became the subjects of Rome. Armenian historiography outlived the independence of Armenia; and Maronite historiography developed in conditions of political subjection.

The answer we can give to our question is perhaps a double one. On the one hand the postbiblical Jews really thought they had in the Bible all the history that mattered: superevalution of a certain type of history implied undervaluation of all other events. On the other hand the whole development of Judaism led to something unhistorical, eternal, the Law, the Torah. The significance which the Jews came to attach to the Torah killed their interest in general historiography. "There is no earlier and no later in the Torah" (*Pes.* 6 b). Indeed, as we all know, "God himself sits and studies the Torah" (*Ab. Zarah* 3 b). Daily acquaintance with the Eternal neither requires nor admits of historical explanations. Life, as regulated by the Torah, presented that formidable simplicity which I was still able to observe in my grandfather, a man famous for piety and learning among Italian Jews. History had nothing to explain and little to reveal to the man who meditated the Law day and night. The Torah is not only permanent in its value, but also regular in its effects. There is something paradoxical in the fact that two of the best writers of autobiography in Antiquity—Ezra and Nehemiah—organised Judaism in such a way as to make history unnecessary. Their fragmentary memoirs have for us the fascination of representing the last steps of a journey towards a world where even history *a contrario*, prophecy, ceases to count, and only the invariable obedience to the Torah remains meaningful.

While the Jewish conception of the Law led to indifference to historical research, the Greek conception of law became an inexhaustible source for historical research in the fifth century B.C. It is no chance that historiography developed in the fifth century in the full maturity of Ionian and Attic democracy. The victory of democracy was the victory for social mobility and reform: it was the victory for free and rational choice. It sharpened the interest in political theories and constitutional changes, it invited comparison between Greek and non-Greek institutions and between the various types of Greek institutions. Modern scholars are inclined to underrate the amount of thought that went into the practical details of constitutional reforms. Because the sixth and fifth centuries were full of constitutional schemes and devices, contemporary historians were made aware of the existing variety of political institutions and social customs. Many constitutional theorists whose names are lost must have existed in Greece in the sixth and fifth centuries. In creating democracy they also created that climate of opinion for which Nomos—Law—became the object of *historia*. The discussion was so far-reaching as to involve a poet like Pindar and a doctor like Hippocrates, not to speak of the historian Herodotus.

Greek Law, Nomos, was not only compatible with historical research but, as understood in the fifth century, and later, proved to be one of the chief ingredients of history writing. The Law of the Jews was definitely beyond History.

VIII

Jewish historiography in the Greek language is no exception, simply because it belongs to Hellenistic, not to Jewish, civilisation. All the nations that came into contact with the Greeks in the Hellenistic age (and even before) produced books in Greek about their national history. They did so partly because the Greeks taught them to see themselves in a different way through the medium of Hellenic *historia*, partly because they wanted to make themselves respectable before Greek eyes. In any case they paid their tribute to an alien civilisation. Jewish writers who wrote in Greek about Jewish history, or indeed any other history, cannot be judged differently. They were making an effort to think in Greek according to Greek categories. The Romans went beyond this stage because they very soon stopped writing in Greek and began to produce historical works in Latin. As a result Greek historiography became part of Latin culture. Sallust, Livy, Tacitus, and Ammianus Marcellinus were the consequences. Today we write history in our respective languages, because the Romans broke the taboo and showed by their example that Greek *historia* could be done in other languages. As far as I know, neither the Eyptians nor the Babylonians nor the Jews ever envisaged that the taboo could be broken. Few or none of them wrote the Greek type of history either in Egyptian or in Babylonian or in Hebrew. For this reason the Jews, unlike the Romans, must be put among the nations which did not assimilate Greek historiography. Historiography of the Greek type never became a recognised part of Jewish life.

There is, however, an important difference between Jews on the one hand and Egyptians or Babylonians on the other. Individual Egyptians or Babylonians acquired the Greek language and could pass for Greeks. But there was never a recognisable variety of Greek civilisation characterised by the fact that it was the product of Greek-speaking Egyptians or Babylonians. By contrast there was a distinctive brand of Hellenism which was Jewish Hellenism. There were entire communities which, even though they considered themselves Jews and practised the Jewish religion, spoke Greek, thought in Greek, and knew hardly any Hebrew or Aramaic. For at least seven or eight centuries Greek remained the alternative cultural language of the Jews. The phenomenon of Jews writing history in Greek is therefore far more important and complicated than the sporadic appearance of Egyptians and Babylonians or Persians writing their own national history in Greek. Some of the Jews who wrote history in Greek were not easily distinguishable from pagans. The Sicilian Jew Caecilius of Calacte wrote about the rebellions of the slaves in Sicily and about the theory of history in a manner acceptable to Dionysius of Halicarnassus and to other pagan members of the educated society of the early first century A.D. A Demetrius of the third century B.C. and an Eupolemus of the second century B.C., who wrote about Jewish history, were taken to be pagans by Josephus. Later Eusebius realised, we do not know how, that they were Jews. No doubt some Jews disguised themselves as pagans in order to be more effective in their propaganda—and some interpolated authentic pagan works, such as those by Manetho and Hecataeus of Abdera, in order to counteract hostile comments by pagans. Other Jews were genuine syncretists who mixed pagan and Jewish elements freely. Artapanus attributed the introduction of Egyptian cults to Moses, and Cleodemus made Hercules the companion of three sons of Abraham. We have no reason to suspect ulterior motives. Others were pious Jews who thought about Jewish history in a Greek literary style, but with few concessions to Greek religious ideas. Jason of Cyrene, whose work on the Maccabean rebellion is summarised in the Second Book of Maccabees, wrote in the tragic style of Hellenistic historiography. As Elias Bickerman showed in his great little book on *Der Gott der Makkabäer*, Jason was more traditional in religious outlook than the author of the Hebrew First Book of Maccabees. He kept to the principle that the fortunes and misfortunes of the Jews entirely depended on their observance of the Law. The author of the First Book of Maccabees was determined to blame the persecutions on the Seleucids. But it would be wrong to regard even Jason as a man who simply presented Jewish ideas in Greek guise. Jason looked upon the Maccabean victory as the fruit of martyrdom. He was the first historian to make martyrdom the centre of his exposition. The importance of his discovery is shown by the place of the Maccabean martyrs in the Christian tradition. The origin of the notion of martyrdom is a notorious subject for controversy. At least it can be said that it was not an exclusively Hebrew notion. Though the Stoic theory of martyrdom is not expounded at length in our sources before Epictetus, Socrates had been the prototype of the philosophic martyr for centuries. The Second Book of Maccabees is at the crossroads between Jewish and Greek thought.

Philo is another historian who cannot be classified either as Greek or as Jew. Only part of his account of contemporary events in Alexandria and Rome has survived, and it is not easy to form an idea of what he wanted to prove. But he operated with elaborate notions, such as those of Pronoia, Arete, and Palinodia, which are not easily translatable into Hebrew. As for Josephus, he was not primarily writing for Hellenised Jews. He was writing for pagans. He wanted to present Jewish history to educated Greek readers and to account for the Jewish war in a way which would be a credit to anyone, including himself and excluding a minority of Jewish fanatics. Nobody to my knowledge has yet explained satisfactorily why and how that strange concoction of the Second Book of Maccabees, of Josephus, and of other writings which we call the Hebrew Josippon came into being in the tenth century and qualified as popular light reading in later centuries. No doubt there was in the ninth and tenth centuries a certain revival of interest in history among the Jews. It began perhaps with a misguided curiosity about the fate of the ten lost tribes which the notorious Eldad-Hadani exploited. Much exploration is needed in these obscure episodes of mediaeval Jewish historiography. New discoveries are not, however, likely to disprove the obvious conclusion that neither II Maccabees, nor Philo, nor Josephus were ever reabsorbed into the Jewish tradition. They remained operative only in Christian learning. II Maccabees, in spirit if not in form, is behind the Christian *Acta Martyrum*. Philo's conception of history is related to that of Lactantius' *De Mortibus Persecutorum*. More generally, Philo is the predecessor of the Christian Platonists. Finally, Josephus is one of the writers without whom Eusebius would not have been able to invent Ecclesiastical History.

Orthodox Judaism was not impervious to Greek influences. The very organisation of traditional Jewish education is inconceivable without the example of the Greek paideia. But history never became part of Jewish education. The Jewish learned man was traditionally a commentator of sacred texts, not a historian. Jewish scholars did not begin to take an interest in the critical reexamination of the Jewish past until the sixteenth century. This was a by-product of the Italian Renaissance. To the extent that the Italian humanists used the methods of Greek philology and history, Jewish scholars also reestablished contact with Greek historical thought. I come almost to family history when I recall the name of Azariah de' Rossi, the scholar from Mantua who gave in the *Me'or 'Enayim* (Light of the Eyes) the first impressive example of the application of Renaissance historical methods to Jewish history. Greek critical methods, if nothing else, were coming back to Judaism by the route of Italy. The next step was the *Tractatus Theologicus-Politicus* by Spinoza.

Spinoza went back to the fundamental principles of Greek historical research in the sense that he treated biblical history as ordinary history in the Greek manner. Furthermore, if it is generally true that Renaissance scholars soon went far beyond what Greek scholars had been able to do in the historical interpretation of ancient texts, this is particularly true of Spinoza. After all he was able to rely on the intimate knowledge of the Bible, and on the sharp observation of details, of generations and generations of Hebrew scholars. He himself was aware of his debt to Ibn Ezra.

Yet not even Spinoza was truly a historian of Judaism. When he said

"dico methodum interpretandi Scripturam haud differre a methodo interpretandi naturam" (*Tract. Theol. Pol.* 7. 6), he certainly reasserted
the principles of free enquiry which had made Greek historiography
possible. But he was interested in eternal truths, not in historical
events. His criticism of the Bible was part of his philosophy, not a contribution to a history of the Jews. He was perhaps none the worse for
that; but the encounter between Spinozism and historical research was
a later development which would have surprised Spinoza himself.

Unlike the Jews the Christians maintained or rather, after an interval, recaptured an interest in history. The expectation of the end of the
world became much more pressing among the Christians than among
the Jews and resulted in the constant scrutiny of events as portents.
Apocalyptic thinking was a stimulus to historical observation. Furthermore—and this was decisive—the conversion of Constantine implied the reconciliation of the majority of the Christian leaders with
the Roman Empire (especially in the East) and gave a precise place
to the Church in mundane affairs. What Christian historians did in
order to justify and clarify these developments will be the subject matter of my last lecture. Here it will be enough to point out that by the
time Christian historiography began in earnest in the third and fourth
centuries A.D., Jewish historiography in Hebrew was a thing of the remote past: and there had been no influential Jewish historian in Greek
after Flavius Josephus. Greek pagan historiography was far more vital
and challenging. Christian ecclesiastical historians, though inevitably
drawing on Daniel and Josephus, ultimately adopted the methods of
pagan historiography—but not, as we shall see, of Greek political
historiography.

CHAPTER TWO

The Herodotean
and the Thucydidean Tradition

I

I hope that my first chapter will at least have made it clear that, though I am capable of any amount of nonsense, I am not so perverse as to deny that the Greeks knew what history was about. When I read "The first thing to remember about the Greek historical consciousness is that it is, in essence, unhistorical" (T. F. Driver, *The Sense of History in Greek and Shakespearean Drama*, Columbia, N.Y., 1960, 19), I ask myself what the critic meant. The notion that the Greek mind was unhistorical has, of course, a respectable pedigree. It goes back through Collingwood and Reinhold Niebuhr to Hegel. It is fashionable among theologians because they are naturally inclined to think that Christianity presents a new and better departure in the understanding of history. Thus we hear that the Greeks were not historically minded because they thought in terms of regular or recurrent patterns, of natural laws, of timeless substance, and so on. Even Greek pessimism is taken to be a proof that the Greeks were incapable of understanding history.

Much of the argument is founded upon vague generalisations about the Greek Mind which betray more familiarity with Pythagoras, Plato, and Zeno the Stoic than with Herodotus, Thucydides, and Polybius. If you identify Plato with the Greek Mind (whatever that may mean), you will conclude that the Greek Mind was not interested in history. In the same way you might conclude that the French Mind is not interested in history because Descartes was a Frenchman. It is an arbitrary generalisation to maintain that Plato is a more typical representative of Greek civilisation than Herodotus. It is another arbitrary

generalisation to maintain that all the Greek and Roman historians believed in regular cycles of human events: Herodotus did not, nor did
Theopompus, Livy, Arrian, and Tacitus. It is yet a further arbitrary
generalisation to maintain that a Christian historian will write better
history than a pagan historian simply because he is a Christian. Herodotus is better than any mediaeval historian I know of with the possible exception of Ibn Khaldun—who was not a Christian and believed
in circular processes of history. The real question is not whether the
Greeks were historically minded, but about the types of history they
wrote and transmitted to us. I begin with political history, but I must
go back to the time when political history had not yet been invented.

At the risk of naivety we must remind ourselves of some basic facts.
Men write history when they want to record events with a chronological framework. Any registration is a selection, and though a selection
of facts does not necessarily imply principles of interpretation, very
often it does. Events may be chosen for registration because they either
explain a change or point to a moral or indicate a recurrent pattern.
Conservation of the memories of the past, a chronological framework,
and an interpretation of the events are elements of historiography to be
found in many civilisations. A Mongolian chronicler of the eighteenth
century is more eloquent about these aspects of history writing than
any Greek historian: "If the common man does not know his origins,
he is like a mad ape. He who does not know his great and right family
connections is like an outsize dragon. He who does not know the circumstances and the course of actions of his noble father and grandfather is like a man who, having prepared sorrow for his children,
throws them into this world."

What I think is typically Greek is the critical attitude towards the
recording of events, that is, the development of critical methods en-
abling us to distinguish between facts and fancies. To the best of my
knowledge no historiography earlier than the Greek or independent of
it developed these critical methods; and we have inherited the Greek
methods.

But the Greek-speaking populations who invaded what we call
Greece in the second millennium B.C. were not provided with a natural
gift for historical criticism. Historical criticism begins in Greece only

in the sixth century B.C., and it would be misleading to suggest that
Homer or Hesiod contributed to the making of what is specific in
Greek historiography. No doubt tales like those of Homer were models
for historical narration. They indicated interest in the past and an extraordinary gift for recalling it. On the other hand genealogical speculations had been a favourite game with the Greeks at least since Hesiod, and probably before him. Thinking in terms of an *arche*, of a
beginning and a development, seems to have been a constant feature of
Greek thought since the beginning. If we knew more about those mysterious compositions which in Hellenistic times circulated as archaic—such as the poem on the early history of Samos attributed to
Semonides of Amorgos (early sixth century?)—we should probably
find some further connection between Homer and the style of the early
Greek historians. But there was no continuity of historical thought
from Hesiod to Hecataeus. At some point between them a revolution
happened. One part of the revolution was political: it was the discovery of the importance of law as a factor of differentiation in human societies. The other part of the revolution was philosophical: the rebellion against tradition, the search for new principles of explanation, the
rise of doubt as an intellectual stimulus to new discoveries.

One name is seldom mentioned when the origins of Greek historiography are studied: the rebel genius of Xenophanes. He refused to
believe in the traditional gods, he emphasised the uncertainty of human knowledge and the relativity of human conceptions. He was interested in discoveries and inventions. He is said to have written poems
about the foundations of Colophon and about the colonisation of Elea:
but the latter at least may be a forgery. He certainly tried to make
guesses about the past of the earth by studying fossils. In an extraordinary fragment we read: "Shells are found inland, and in the moun-
tains, and in the quarries in Syracuse . . . an impression of a fish and
of a seaweed has been found, while an impression of a bay leaf was
found in Paros in the depth of the rock, and in Malta flat shapes of all
marine objects" (fr. 187 Kirk–Raven). Thucydides adopted a method
singularly reminiscent of this study of fossils when he examined the
surviving customs of past ages in Greece. Xenophanes implies in a
poem that he has already lived ninety-two years. His life must have ex-

tended from about 560 to about 470: the century in which Hecataeus reached maturity and Herodotus was a boy.

Xenophanes does not seem to have undertaken any systematic revision of the Greek historical tradition or to have formulated any criterion about its validity. Yet by questioning the traditional opinions about the gods, he made inevitable the examination of that part of Greek history which was the borderland between gods and men. Hecataeus, the subtle and ruthless Milesian who reluctantly took a leading part in the Ionian rebellion between 500 and 494 B.C., undertook that examination. He wrote about the geography of the earth and the genealogies of the Greeks. He used the results of extensive research in Oriental lands, and especially in Phoenicia and Egypt, to show that Greek myths were untenable because they went against established facts of Oriental chronology. The best-known story about him is reported by Herodotus (II, 143). He boasted to the priests of an Egyptian temple that he could count sixteen ancestors, and the sixteenth was a god. That amounted to putting the heroic age sixteen generations before 500 B.C. The answer of the Egyptian priests was to introduce Hecataeus to the images of 345 generations of their predecessors—priests after priests, and no trace of god or hero at the beginning.

A man who wished to adhere to the tradition of his own family would have no difficulty in meeting the challenge of the Egyptian priests. He would have replied that evidently the gods had kept longer in direct contact with the Greeks than with the Egyptians. But Hecataeus was in no such mood. The lesson he derived is stated in the introduction to one of his two works—the *Genealogies*. In words which have not yet lost their force after 2,500 years he proclaimed: "I Hecataeus will say what I think to be the truth; the stories of the Greeks are many and ridiculous." The new attitude towards tradition is plain. One has simply to compare it with that of Hesiod. Hesiod knew that he was fallible. He sang what the Muses told him, and he was aware that the Muses did not always tell the truth. But he had no way of checking the inspiration he had received from them.

Hecataeus did find an objective criterion for a choice between facts and fancies. He was no longer at the mercy of the Muses. He turned to foreign evidence. By comparison with the non-Greek tradition,

Greek tradition was shown to be "ridiculous." The enlargement of the geographical horizon resulted also in an extension of the chronological framework of tradition, with disastrous results for the Greek measurements of the past. Besides, Hecataeus pointedly mentioned the multiplicity of Greek tales. The Greek "logoi" were "many" *and* "ridiculous." He seems to imply that the Greek traditions, there being so many, contradicted each other and added to their own absurdity.

So much, I think, is fairly clear. But the extant fragments do not allow us to see what was Hecataeus' next step. Did he conclude that at least certain Greek gods and heroes were a fiction? Or did he consign the Greek gods to the chronological level of the Egyptian gods? In the latter case did he suggest that the Greeks established their chronology on the basis of a confusion between later human namesakes of the gods and the real gods? The answer depends to a very large extent on how much of Hecataeus we are prepared to find in Herodotus. Herodotus certainly distinguished in Book II a Hercules who was a god from a later Hercules who was a hero. And there are various good reasons for believing that when he wrote Book II about Egypt he was under the spell of his predecessor. But it is obviously hazardous to ascribe to Hecataeus those opinions in Herodotus' Book II which look strongly rationalistic. The fragments we can confidently attribute to Hecataeus only suggest that he saw nothing superhuman in the ordinary tales about Hercules. Other fragments show the same tendency to criticise tradition by doing away with the dog Cerberus and by reducing in number the sons of Aegyptus. The limits and methods of this rationalisation of the myths are not easy to see. In one case at least Hecataeus reported tradition and then commented: "Ridiculous and unbelievable, yet this is what they say" (fr. 328 Jacoby). Apparently in this case he did not feel able to offer an alternative version of his own.

We shall be wise not to try to force the evidence for Hecataeus into some coherent pattern. We do not know whether he was prepared to deny the existence of the gods of Greek religion, though his thoughts seem to have run in that direction. He did not refuse credence to unusual experiences and what we should call miracles, as long as they were not adduced in support of traditional myths. The general trend of his criticism seems to have been to attribute to men what tradition attributed to gods. The real importance of Hecataeus is not in the individual interpretations he propounded but in the discovery that a systematic criticism of historical tradition is both possible and desirable, and that a comparison between different national traditions helps to establish the truth.

The situation in which he lived compelled him paradoxically to become a leader of the Ionian rebellion against the Persians; but he never ceased to be a *philo-barbaros*. Heraclitus disliked him perhaps for the same reason that Hegel disliked B. G. Niebuhr. The conservative thinker had little sympathy with the empirical researcher of a more liberal outlook. Hecataeus, by his erudition, made nonsense of the claims of Greek aristocrats like Heraclitus to be descendants of gods. Hecataeus' admiration for the barbarians had political undertones, just as there were political undertones in Niebuhr's admiration for the Roman peasants.

II

Hecataeus acted in the Ionian rebellion, but we have no reason to believe that he wrote about it. The idea of extending historical criticism from the remote past to the recent past does not seem to have occurred to him. His type of analysis was not that of a man who knows the difficulties of collecting the evidence, but that of a man who presupposes the evidence to be known. He started by declaring that the tales of the Greeks were many and ridiculous. His successor Herodotus began with the declaration that it was his purpose to preserve from decay the recollection of what men had done and to prevent the great and marvellous actions of the Greeks and of the barbarians from forgoing their due tribute of glory. Like every other Greek, Herodotus was concerned with the ephemeral character of human actions. Like many other Greeks he believed that memory of past deeds was the only (imperfect) remedy man had at his disposal against his own mortality. At first sight the programme appears to be a Homeric one; indeed without Homer, Herodotus could never have conceived it. Yet the historian was on his guard. He knew that his task was twofold: to preserve tradition was necessary, but to find out the truth about it was equally desirable.

He realised that poets sing of events that never happened, and he was not prepared to bestow immortality on what had never come into being.

The old theory that Herodotus set out as a geographer in Hecataeus' first manner and only slowly developed the idea of writing a history of the Persian Wars still seems to me plausible. At least it emphasises the undoubted fact that a history of the Persian Wars was something Herodotus had to discover for himself, while descriptions of foreign countries existed before him. But the development of Herodotus is less important to us than his final stand. Ultimately Herodotus determined to take responsibility for the registration of events and traditions that had not yet been recorded in writing. At the same time, he extended the scope of his criticism to examine both the very ancient and the fairly recent, both the Greek and the foreign. The implications of his decision were enormous.

The instrument of criticism used by Hecataeus had never been very precise. Used as it was by Herodotus for all sorts of traditions, it was bound to become even less precise. The simple expedient of comparison was hardly adequate when Herodotus came to question the validity both of the Greek and of the non-Greek traditions. Nor did he find it so easy to reduce the traditional tales to ordinary human terms when he had to face foreign myths. Besides, the burning fire of incredulity was absent in him. He refrained from saying certain things because it would have been offensive to the gods to say them (II, 3; 61). In one case he added: "Having said so much may I incur no displeasure of either god or hero" (II, 45). His religious scruples were in tune with his dislike of any utterance that would give away inner feelings or would seem to be ostentatiously in favour of one side against the other. With characteristic diffidence and elaborate precautions he stated that Athens had saved Greece during the Persian Wars (VII, 139). In other arguments, both religious and profane, he admitted that he spoke only because impelled to do so by the trend of his discourse (II, 65; VII, 96, 99). It is difficult to imagine a man more temperamentally different from Hecataeus than Herodotus. It is arguable that the historian from Halicarnassus reflected the soberer mood of Greece after the Persian Wars. If he wrote mainly in Athens, Sophocles, who was his friend,

may have taught him something about the mysterious ways of gods
and the vain pretences of men.

Herodotus' reactions to the stories he heard are unpredictable, un-
systematic, and partly self-contradictory. He cannot believe that the
Neuri became wolves once a year, though the Greeks of Scythia state
this under oath (IV, 105). Nor does he believe that Scyllias of Scion
swam eighty stages under water to desert to the Greeks (VIII, 8). But
he can tell the story of how Alcmeon filled himself with gold at Croe-
sus' expense without interposing a word of caution (VI, 125). In certain cases he decides to indicate that there was more than one version
to his tale. He gives both the better and the worse versions of a detail
of Cambyses' march through the Syrian desert, and he hints at conflicting details about the death of Polycrates (III, 122). He also tells at
length both the Sybarite and the Crotoniate versions of Dorieus' intervention in the affairs of the Italian Greeks (V, 44–45) and leaves the
reader to judge which is preferable. But to all appearances he is not
consistent in reporting conflicting versions.

If we had to assess Herodotus simply as a follower of Hecataeus'
method, we should have to consider him inferior to his master. There
are modern critics who have reached this conclusion. But Herodotus
clearly goes beyond Hecataeus both in the matter of principles and in
the matter of interests. The two principles to which Herodotus remained consistently faithful are not to be found in Hecataeus. The first
is the duty to give priority to recording over criticising. As he says on
one occasion: "For myself, though it be my business to set down that
which is told me, to believe it is none at all of my business; let that
saying hold good for the whole of my history" (VII, 152). The second
principle is the separation of what he has seen with his own eyes from
what he has heard: "Thus far all I have said is the outcome of my own
sight and judgment and inquiry. Henceforth I will record Egyptian
chronicles, according to that which I have heard, adding thereto somewhat of what I myself have seen" (II, 99). In making this distinction
between what he has seen and what he has heard, Herodotus is precise
sometimes to the point of pedantry. For instance, he tells us that when
he visited the labyrinth near Lake Moeris he was allowed to see the up-
per chambers, but not the lower chambers (II, 148). In other cases,

when he reports from somebody else's account, he takes trouble to indicate the degree of reliability of his informants. He went all the way
to Heliopolis because the local priests had the reputation of being the
most competent—λογιώτατοι—among the Egyptians (II, 3). He also
likes to state that a certain report appears to him very reliable. The emphasis on the trustworthiness of his information is one of the most
characteristic features of Herodotus' critical method.

Now, when Herodotus took the recording of tradition as his primary duty, he was in fact doing something more than simply saving
facts from oblivion. He was guiding historical research towards the exploration of the unknown and of the forgotten. Hecataeus' method in
his book on genealogies, as far as it is known to us, was mainly concerned with criticism of the known. Herodotus went to foreign countries to discover historical events. At the same time, he developed a distinction between things seen and things heard that was essential to the
new type of exploration. Unlike Hecataeus he was no longer primarily
a judge of what he heard but a discoverer of new facts. Therefore he
had to indicate which of the reports he could vouch for. The task of
preserving traditions implied the aim of discovering new facts. Both together entailed a new methodical approach in which the reliability of
evidence mattered more than rational evaluation of probabilities. Hecataeus' method was not discarded, though Herodotus was occasionally impatient with his predecessor. But for the purpose of establishing
the truth the cross-examination of witnesses became more important
than the rational justification of a theory. A characteristic example are
those chapters of Book IV in which Herodotus criticises Hecataeus'
theory about the Hyperboreans with unusual sarcasm (IV, 32ff.). Part
of the criticism is on the ordinary levels of probability, as we would expect from a pupil of Hecataeus. But the main line of the argument is
an examination of the authority of the various witnesses.

By combining enquiry with criticism of the evidence, Herodotus extended the limits of historical research to embrace the greater part of
the world as then known. In such a complex enquiry chronology became a major problem. He had to build up a chronological framework
capable of including several different national traditions which had
never been brought together before and for which there was no com-

mon measure of time. It is the merit of Professor H. Strasburger to have
shown how skilfully and unassumingly Herodotus created his chronology. By implying in VIII, 51, 1, that Kalliades was the archon in
Athens in the sixth year after the death of Darius, when Xerxes went
to Greece, he constructed the bridge between Oriental and Greek chronology that still holds good after 2,400 years.

The other problem was how to collect the evidence when written
records were not accessible or did not exist. As for the Eastern countries, Herodotus was deprived of direct access to chronicles and other
documents by his ignorance both of the languages and of their scripts.
In Greece written documents were few and for the most part concealed
in the archives of temples and cities, out of a visitor's reach except by
special favour. It is clear that Herodotus must have had access to certain documents in Greek concerning Persian taxation (III, 89), the Persian royal road (V, 52), and the Persian ships (VII, 89; VIII, 66; VIII,
130). For a few inscriptions in hieroglyphics and cuneiform he depended on translations provided for him by local guides and interpreters. The best known examples are the inscriptions of the pyramids (II,
125) and those of Sesostris (II, 102). As for the Greeks, Hecataeus is
the only contemporary prose writer whom we know Herodotus to
have used. Aeschylus is the only contemporary poet from whom he
took over some facts. All the other literary quotations come from poets
of the past. He knew so many oracles that one may suspect he found
them already collected together in a book. The Greek chronicles and
memoirs which are put forward from time to time as sources of Herodotus have never been more than vague shadows: the Delphic chronicle once advocated by Wilamowitz and the memoirs of Dikaios are
now discredited. Greek inscriptions Herodotus read for himself,
though one can be in some doubt as to what he made of the "Cadmean
letters" he saw in the temple of the Ismenian Apollo at Thebes (V, 59).
He quotes only twelve Greek inscriptions and another dozen foreign
documents. If the so-called decree of Themistocles discovered at Troe-
zene is authentic, it is a splendid example of the kind of document Herodotus never saw. He did not know that, according to this decree,
only half the Athenian fleet was meant to face the Persians at the Artemisium. Furthermore, he puts the decision to evacuate Athens after

the battle of the Artemisium, whereas the decree would imply that it was taken before it. But perhaps he did not know the decree simply because the decree did not yet exist when he wrote.

Altogether it is clear that Herodotus elected to build his story mainly on oral evidence and that his very method rests on oral rather than on written evidence. He mentions many of his informants, but does not give the impression that those he chooses to name are the most important. One wonders, for instance, what he gleaned from Zopyrus son of Megabyzus, who deserted from the Persians to Athens and who received special mention in his work (III, 160). The study of the technique whereby Herodotus collected and organised his evidence during his travels is still in its infancy. This technique demanded a well-developed memory and cannot be separated from the more intangible qualities that made Herodotus the unique man he was. There is no definition for the gifts of curiosity, patience, and humanity that Herodotus brought to his enquiry. He never rejoiced over fallen enemies, never celebrated power as power, never dictated history its course. He was invariably attentive to individual situations. Though careful to note similarities, he was even readier to detect differences; and there is not one scene in his work that looks like another. If there is transcendent teaching in his tale, it is that of measure in all things. Herodotus' method is that of a man who does not want to suppress what is not in his power to understand or to correct and who allows mankind—or its greater part—to reflect itself undisturbed in his mirror.

III

The importance of Herodotus' achievement was very soon recognised. He made an impression on his contemporaries Sophocles and Aristophanes. He was given a handsome present by the Athenians for his pro-Athenian writings, as we are told by an apparently reliable source, Diyllus (fr. 3 Jacoby). His popularity with the Athenians was remarkable, seeing he was the man who had observed, with direct reference to Athens, that it was easier to fool thirty thousand men than one. He was acknowledged to have been the father of history—an appellation at least as old as Cicero. He was summarised by Theopompus

and commented upon by Aristarchus. Yet his reputation was never
that of the truthful historian. Even those who admired him most, such
as Dionysius of Halicarnassus and Lucian, praised his style rather than
his reliability. Thucydides expressed his contempt for the levity of his
predecessor, and the opinion of the succeeding centuries was on the
whole on his side. Ctesias and Aristotle, Diodorus, Strabo, and Plutarch threw mud at Herodotus, and many were the books and pam-
phlets to denounce his lies. Even in the fourth century A.D., Libanius
felt obliged to write against Herodotus. His method quite clearly failed
to persuade. His readers could not believe that he was telling the truth.
One can argue that the failure was due in part to his shortcomings. He
did not draw a clear line between what he reported and what he accepted as true. But any careful reader ought to have realised that he did
not take responsibility for all the stories he told. Moreover, the sheer
magnitude of his enterprise should have commanded respect. The hostility towards Herodotus is something more than a theoretical distrust
of a method. The critics were not capable of appreciating the depth of
his humanity and the subtlety of his reactions. The critic we know best,
Plutarch, disliked Herodotus because he was not patriotic enough and
had preferred Athens to Boeotia.

Herodotus would not have suffered such a fate if Thucydides had
not given a new turn to historical studies that involved a repudiation
of his predecessor. The factors which contributed to Herodotus' discredit were many, but one stands out: Thucydides put himself between
Herodotus and his readers. The exploration of the wider world was
not Thucydides' vocation. He was an exile for at least twenty years.
There were not many men he liked in Athens, and anyway he was not
born to love his fellow beings. Yet every word he spoke was that of an
Athenian. All his intellectual energies were directed towards understanding the meaning of the war he had to face as an Athenian. He saw
no escape from the polis in which he was born simply because he conceived life in terms of political life and history in terms of political history. Even the plague—the only extrapolitical experience he could not
avoid—is eventually examined for its political consequences. Thucydides' reaction against Herodotus has its ultimate justification in a disagreement about what is historical certainty, but was primarily due to

the revulsion of a man committed to the political life against a good-humoured cosmopolitan. Had not Herodotus treated as a joke the return of Pisistratus led by a woman masquerading as Athena?: "Seeing that from old times the Hellenic has ever been distinguished from the Barbarian stock by its greater cleverness and its freedom from silly foolishness, [it is strange] that these men should devise such a plan to deceive the Athenians, said to be the most cunning of the Greeks" (I, 60).

Thucydides had the same questioning mind as his contemporaries the Sophists, but he concentrated exclusively on political life. The past was to him the mere beginning of the political situation that existed in the present; and the present was the basis for understanding the past. If one understands the present, one understands the workings of human nature. Present experiences can be put to future uses (though the details of such utilisation are left uncertain) or, alternatively, are the key to the past. Thucydides assumes that the differences between different ages are more quantitative than qualitative. Human nature remains fundamentally the same. But the present is the only period about which it is possible to have reliable information, and therefore historical research must start with the present and can go into the past only as far as the evidence allows. So strong is Thucydides' conviction about the centrality of the present in historical research that he does not feel it necessary to examine at length the complementary proposition that the present is the only time for which reliable information is available. The unique position of contemporary history depends on the double assumption that there is something immutable in human nature and that contemporary history is the only history which can be told reliably. The further premise that the events to be reckoned with are political narrows down the selection of significant facts even in the present. Men want power, and can achieve it only within the state. Internal feuds and external wars are the result. Mere biography is by definition excluded: man's action is either political or nothing. But man's action is not invariably blind. In times of revolution passions can reach the point at which individuals are no longer able to answer for their actions. All that the historian can do in these circumstances is to define the mechanism of their passions—which Thucydides does in the famous chapters of Book III. Normally, however, the political leaders can explain themselves. No ordinary struggle for power can be understood without taking into account what leaders say. Indeed it is the special responsibility of the political leader to show his grasp of the situation in speeches which persuade the crowd without making concessions to its blind passions. The historian will therefore take as much care to remember what leaders say as to record what they do. But he also knows that it is more difficult to give a trustworthy rendering of a speech than a precise picture of a military expedition.

It is a notoriously open question whether Thucydides meant to convey the real utterances of the orators or whether his speeches represented their hidden thoughts rather than their actual orations. Put in this crude way, the problem is insoluble. Any reader of Thucydides has to admit that certain speeches look improbable. The debate between Cleon and Diodotus about the treatment of the Mytileneans in Book III is an example. The dialogue between Athenians and Melians in Book V is another. The relative uniformity of the structure of the various speeches is a further difficulty for those who take them as a faithful record of what was said. On the other hand there is no a priori reason to doubt that at least in Athens men with a sophisticated education could speak in the way in which Thucydides makes them speak. The truth must lie somewhere beyond the two opposite interpretations of Thucydides' speeches. He intended to report real speeches and knew how difficult it was to do so. But judging politicians as he did by their grasp of the situation, he had to indicate what they must have thought, even in cases where they were likely to have spoken differently.

Like Herodotus, Thucydides did not question the presupposition that oral tradition was more important than the written one. Like Herodotus he first trusted his own eyes and ears and next the eyes and ears of reliable witnesses. A casual remark in Book VII (44) shows how well he realised the limited value of eyewitnesses in battles. In two ways, however, he differed from Herodotus. First of all, he was never satisfied with straightforward reporting without taking responsibility for what he reported. Mere λέγω τὰ λεγόμενα was not for him. Second (and the second point is to a certain extent a consequence of the first), he very seldom indicated the sources of his information in detail. He

felt he should be taken on trust. Having imposed such severe geographical and chronological limits on his enterprise, he thought he could go
to his readers and ask them to believe him. It never occurred to him
that it could be otherwise.

Very little of his history is built on written evidence. Furthermore,
at least some of the documents he quotes are not used to prove anything in particular but are simply part of the story. This explains, as I
have already mentioned in my first chapter, why Wilamowitz and E.
Schwartz thought that if Thucydides had completed his work he would
have replaced the original text of these documents by a paraphrase in
his own style. The suggestion is interesting but hardly convincing. In
other cases Thucydides quotes, or alludes to, texts with the clear purpose of proving a point. Such texts are all concerned with past history
and are to be found in excursuses. The letters exchanged between Pausanias and the King of Persia (I, 128), the first draft of the inscription
on the tripod of Delphi (I, 132, 2), and the stele indicating where Pausanias was buried are mentioned in order to authenticate and explain
the story (I, 134, 4). The monument to Themistocles in the market-
place of Magnesia is mentioned (I, 138, 5) to confirm that Themistocles was a governor of the city on behalf of the Persians—it is also a
fact in contrast to the rumour, for which Thucydides cannot vouch,
that Themistocles' bones had been transported to Athens and secretly
buried in Attica.

The use of documents and monuments in the excursuses is to be compared with that of the "proofs," or τεκμήρια, in the introduction—
the so-called Archaeology. Here again Thucydides deals with the past,
indeed with a much more remote past. He realises that he must make
conjectures based on evidence. The evidence he uses is of different
kinds: a passage from Homer, a present-day custom interpreted as a
survival, or even an archaeological datum, such as that provided by the
tombs of Delos (I, 8, 1). In one case it is fairly certain that Thucydides
must have used a local chronicle from Samos. A method which combines archaeological data, comparative ethnography, and historical
interpretation of literary texts seems to us so good that we wonder why
Thucydides used it only in his preface. The explanation is obvious.
Thucydides does not describe the past as he describes the present.

What seems to us the surest method of historical research is for Thucydides a second best to replace direct observation when certain and detailed knowledge is impossible. The past for Thucydides is not interesting or significant in itself. It is only the prelude to the present. The development from past to present is a linear one. As Mme. de Romilly has observed, Thucydides "prête à l'histoire une progression allant toujours dans le même sens" (*Histoire et raison chez Thucydide*, 1956, 294). To put it more pointedly, just because the past leads by simple progression to the present, the only way of knowing about it is to go back from the present. This is another difference with Herodotus, for whom the past was significant in itself.

IV

It is difficult to say how much Thucydides impressed his immediate successors in the fourth century B.C. Philistus of Syracuse, who is described as his closest follower, is little more than a name to us. Cratippus, who is said to have continued his work, is also mentioned as a critic of Thucydides' speeches. If Cratippus is the author of the *Hellenica Oxyrhynchia* something more can be said about him: he was objective and careful and followed Thucydides in chronology and in distinguishing between superficial and profound causes of events. Xenophon and Theopompus started where Thucydides had stopped, but their points of view were very different. Xenophon thought that the Spartans had lost the hegemony over Greece because the gods punished them after their treacherous capture of the citadel of Thebes. One wonders what Thucydides would have thought of that. Theopompus developed a highly emotional approach to Athenian politics and, generally speaking, took sides in a way that was repugnant to Thucydides. Ephorus went back to earlier times and covered that period between the Trojan and the Peloponnesian wars which Thucydides had not considered the proper field for detailed research. Thucydides did not impress his successors when he claimed that the study of contemporary history reveals permanent features of human nature. The historians of the fourth century preferred the simpler view (which they transmitted to the succeeding centuries) that history is a lesson in behaviour. Nor did they share his virtual atheism or his impassioned evaluation of human events in terms of conflicts of power. What is perhaps more important, these fourth-century historians tried to do something which Thucydides had not done. Xenophon experimented with intellectual biography, with philosophic historiography, and with straight autobiography (the account of his military experiences in the *Anabasis*). Theopompus (I would still maintain even after Professor Connor's book) placed one man, Philip of Macedon, at the centre of the great picture of contemporary life in his *Philippic Histories*. Ephorus tried to write Greek history from the origins within the framework of a universal history; Polybius considered Ephorus to be his predecessor as a universal historian.

Yet very few doubted either in the fourth century or later that Thucydides was trustworthy. Only Flavius Josephus mentions in passing that there were critics of Thucydides' reliability. On the whole Thucydides remained the model of the truthful historian. Thucydides saved history from becoming the prey of the increasingly influential rhetoricians who cared more for words than for truth. When Praxiphanes, the pupil of Theophrastus, wrote a dialogue to explain what history is about, he chose Thucydides as the model historian. Even Thucydides' principle that contemporary history is more reliable than past history was not seriously questioned. Ephorus himself, who broke away from contemporary history, admitted in the preface to his work that it was impossible to be as reliably informed about the past as about recent events. The most important achievement of Thucydides was to persuade his successors that history is political history. None of the great historians of the fourth century really departed from this notion. Geography in the Herodotean sense and extrapolitical events do appear in historical works of the fourth century, but in the form of introductions to real history or in excursuses. Ephorus had a geographical introduction; Theopompus indulged in a long excursus on prodigies and had another, of slanderous biographical character, on demagogues. The main line of both Ephorus and Theopompus was political.

In later centuries Thucydides was often discussed and criticised as a writer. It is enough to read the life of Thucydides written by Mar-

cellinus or the rhetorical treatises of Dionysius of Halicarnassus to discover the main criticisms that were levelled against him. Dionysius,
who resented Thucydides' obscurities, went so far as to rewrite whole
passages to show how Thucydides should have expressed himself. The
controversy about Thucydides' style penetrated to Rome in the wake
of Atticism and became part of Roman literary life from the time of
Sallust and Cicero. There were always people who preferred Herodotus to Thucydides in the matter of style, and there was equally a good
number of historians from Arrian to Procopius who eclectically imitated Herodotean and Thucydidean features of language. But what
happened to Herodotus never happened to Thucydides: that those
who admired his style declared him a liar. Nor did those who used him
most proclaim him unreliable. Unlike Ctesias and Manetho in the case
of Herodotus, Ephorus and Aristotle did not insult Thucydides after
having used him. The influence of Herodotus as a historian, as a master of historical method, is something to be discovered with difficulty
and almost entirely indirectly. We may suspect it in the wide view Timaeus took of his history of the West; we may more certainly perceive
it in the structure of Posidonius' histories, a continuation of Polybius.
Where ethnography combined with history in the description of foreign nations, as in Megasthenes' description of India and in Hecataeus
of Abdera's account of Egypt, the Greek historians maintained contact
with the teaching of Herodotus; and so did the foreigners who came
to write the history of their own nations according to Greek methods.
But even these historians had difficulty in combining military-political
history with descriptions of lands and customs in the manner of Herodotus. To give the most obvious example, Arrian separated his account of India from his history of Alexander the Great. The historians
of Greece, the writers of monographs about individual Greek states,
about Alexander and his successors, remained constant to pure political and military history. Political history—"Thucydidean" history—
continued to be the history par excellence for the majority of the
ancients.

Ethnography, biography, religion, economics, art, when touched
upon at all, remained marginal. The most serious historians of the Hellenistic period and many who were not serious confined themselves to
wars and alliances. Ptolemy and Aristobulos among the historians of

Alexander, Hieronymus of Cardia among the memorialists of the next generation, were political historians. This trend was given new authority by Polybius. The Roman senators who educated themselves on Thucydides and Polybius were of course inclined, if anything, to accentuate the unilaterality of the political and military approach. The case of Polybius deserves particular attention both in itself and for the influence it had on Greek and Roman historiography. He admired Ephorus more than Thucydides. This is natural enough in a universal historian. As far as I know, Thucydides is mentioned only once in the surviving parts of Polybius (VIII, 11, 3), and not in a very significant context. Polybius' strictly didactic attitude towards history is very different from that of Thucydides. In his statements about speeches one may detect an implicit criticism of the obviously invented speeches of Thucydides: he wants historians to report speeches as they were actually made. Yet Polybius accepts all the fundamentals of Thucydides' method. He accepts Thucydides' notion of historical truth, his distinction between profound and superficial causes (though he may use a different terminology), and, above all, his notion of political and contemporary history. He may not have admired Thucydides, but he certainly learned a lot from him. He kept history writing in the direction indicated by Thucydides. By demolishing Timaeus in the ruthless way he did, Polybius eliminated one of the first-rank Hellenistic historians in whom one could see a clear trace of Herodotean methods. He had a decisive effect in persuading the Romans that history is mainly political history. This persuasion was not entirely superfluous. However inclined we may be to take the Romans as political animals, the first Roman historian, Fabius Pictor, was not averse to the nonpolitical aspects of history. His model was Timaeus. He may never have read Thucydides. Nor did Cato commit himself to a purely political history. But the next generations of Roman historians who read Polybius were won over to a strict ideal of political history: we find it in Sallust as much as in Livy and Tacitus. Cicero remembered Thucydides when he said that the first law of history is to say nothing more and nothing less than the truth, "Nam quis nescit primam esse historiae legem, ne quid falsi dicere audeat, deinde ne quid veri non audeat" (*De orat.* II, 15, 62).

It is interesting that outside Republican Rome Polybius never shared the prestige of Thucydides. The Greeks—even the Greeks who wrote about Rome in the Imperial age, such as Dio Cassius—recognised that Thucydides, not Polybius, was the model of political history. Style more than contents, one suspects, determined their preference. No writer of the second century B.C. had any chance of competing with the "classics" in the schools of the Imperial age. Yet it was not only a question of style. As long as readers were told that Herodotus was a liar and Thucydides was the truth, Thucydides was bound to remain the ideal representative of history. Lucian stated this in words which Ranke must have known well. It was Thucydides, according to Lucian, who gave history its law—the law of saying ὡς ἐπράχθη, what had been done (25, 41). Lucian added that Thucydides enacted this law against Herodotus. We may well feel disappointed in the quality of the work done by the pupils of Thucydides in Antiquity. None had his penetrating intelligence, very few had his aristocratic sincerity and soberness of judgement. We shall not discuss here why men of genius are not more frequent. Certain other reasons for the decline in quality after Thucydides are apparent. The climate of intellectual liberty of fifth-century Athens was unique. From the fourth century B.C. rhetoric attracted the historians, and philosophy dissuaded them from history. Finally, a historiography that is compelled to deal with the past with inadequate instruments is bound to be very sensitive to political pressures and unable to rethink the past in depth. Some of these limitations, as we shall see, remained operative until the nineteenth century. But it would be hard to underrate the amount of sober and permanent work done by historians in the wake of Thucydides. A few of their new lines I have already indicated. I cannot subscribe to my friend M. I. Finley's judgement: "Of all the lines of inquiry which the Greeks initiated, history was the most abortive" (Introd. to *The Greek Historians*, New York, 1959, 20).

V

If we pass from Antiquity to the Renaissance, our first impression is that Polybius counted for more than Thucydides. He is indeed the first Greek historian to have made a big impact on the Westerners who had rediscovered the Greek historians. His subject matter was far more interesting and familiar to the humanists than the obscure Peloponnesian War. He was paraphrased by Leonardo Bruni, studied by Politian, commented upon by Machiavelli. Polybius, together with Livy and Tacitus, is behind the revival of the Greek ideal of political history that is such a conspicuous part of the more general renaissance of classical values and forms in the sixteenth century. Until the end of the seventeenth century Polybius remained the master of political, diplomatic, and military wisdom. Casaubon was his translator and his apologist. Justus Lipsius, the commentator and champion of Tacitus, was also a great student of Polybius as a military historian, whom he treated as a good guide in fighting the Turks. Isaac Vossius put him at the centre of Greek historiography. In comparison with him Thucydides attracted positive attention as a historian in select circles. The authoritative criticisms by Dionysius of Halicarnassus were heeded. The translator and commentator of Dionysius on Thucydides, Andreas Dudith, was also the most acrimonious enemy of Thucydides in the sixteenth century: "Non iam in historia summus Thucydides videbitur sed . . . postremo in ordine contemptus iacebit." It did not help much that Lucian—whose pamphlet on history was compulsory reading in the Renaissance—was a great admirer of Thucydides. The few who were interested in Thucydides were not professional historians. Hobbes was not, nor was the Jesuit Père Rapin (1681). They represented the tastes of men who wanted a more candid and subtle view of human nature than that offered by Polybius and Tacitus. Père Rapin knew his Pascal and Corneille. But the very fact that his defence of Thucydides took the form of a comparison between Thucydides and Livy—and the result was left in doubt—shows that Rapin was not interested in historical research.

It was not until the second part of the eighteenth century, as far as I know, that the general climate of opinion began to change to the definite advantage of Thucydides. The Abbé de Mably commended Thucydides as the historian whom princes and their ministers should read once a year (*De la manière d'écrire l'histoire*, 1784, 125). Then the Romantic movement elevated Thucydides to the position which he still occupies and made him the model philosophic historian, who com-

bines accurate examination of details with a deep imaginative understanding of the working of the human mind. Thucydides, though exact, was not a pedant, and the pedants were now growing as fast as the
Monumenta Germaniae. There is an element of nostalgia in the
nineteenth-century cult for Thucydides which we have inherited. The
view that obtained in Creuzer, Schelling, F. Schlegel, and Ranke found
its most attractive formulation in the Life of Thucydides by W.
Roscher, a pupil of Ranke and one of the founders of modern eco-
nomic studies. All these people opposed Thucydides to Polybius as the
artistic to the inartistic, the philosophic to the utilitarian. Those who
wanted to defend Polybius had to point out that he was more of a universal historian than Thucydides and therefore nearer to Christianity.
Even so, few were convinced by this observation, which was made for
instance by H. Ulrici in his excellent *Charakteristik der antiken His-
toriographie* (1833).

To us, however, the conflict between Thucydides and Polybius in the
early nineteenth century is less interesting than another aspect of the
change in the fortunes of Thucydides. It was Herodotus who rescued
Thucydides at the eleventh hour. Thucydides' admirers were by now
also, primarily, Herodotus' admirers. They admired Thucydides for
qualities they had first encountered in Herodotus. The conflict between
Thucydides and Polybius had come to replace the conflict between Herodotus and Thucydides. Critics began to discover harmony between
Herodotus and Thucydides—or at least acknowledged that they com-
plemented each other. What had happened?

What happened, broadly speaking, was that since the middle of the
sixteenth century Herodotus had become a very respectable and a very
respected author. When he had started to circulate again in the West
in about 1460, in Valla's translation, the humanists of course remembered the old attacks against him. For a while they were divided in
their loyalties. Should one believe the ancients who called Herodotus
a liar, or should one abandon oneself to the charm and the doctrine of
the newly revealed author? Pontano had tried to strike a balance, J. L.
Vives had made Herodotus an occasion for attacks against the Greek
liars of every age. But there were two new factors: America had been
discovered; and the Reformation had created a new interest in biblical

history. In America the Europeans could see many things more incredible than those they read in Herodotus, and incidentally Herodotus was a great help in trying to describe them. Furthermore, no one but Herodotus could help to fill the background of Oriental history necessary for an understanding of biblical history. Henricus Stephanus in his *Apologia pro Herodoto* of about 1566 was the first to grasp the impact of the new geographical discoveries on the evaluation of Herodotus. Scaliger, on the other hand, admired and used Herodotus as a supplement to the Bible. Later in the seventeenth century Herodotus was used to defend Bible stories which the sceptics were beginning to doubt. When men like Newton declared their faith in Herodotus, respectability was assured. Newton declared that he drew up chronological tables to "make chronology suit with the course of nature, with astronomy, with sacred history and with Herodotus, the father of history." This, historiographically, had profound consequences. It meant that modern ethnography was born as a conscious continuation of the work done by Herodotus and the other geographers and ethnographers of Antiquity. As Herodotus, among the surviving authors of Antiquity, had travelled most—even more than Polybius—and had derived least from preexisting books, he became an inspiration to the true traveller as opposed to the armchair historian. But Herodotus was more than that. He was the candid, poetic historian who believed in some sort of divine intervention in human affairs, talked pleasantly about freedom, respected and loved popular traditions. On the eve of Romanticism, Herder was not slow to perceive that Herodotus was his ally. Herodotus had "the effortless, mild sense of humanity," "der unangestrengte, milde Sinn der Menschheit," and Herder's words were echoed by many other critics in the late eighteenth and early nineteenth centuries. When Voltaire tried to superimpose an "histoire des mœurs" on the ordinary history of battles, who could provide a better example than Herodotus? Admittedly Herodotus was naive, but here Thucydides could act as a corrective, both in realism and in accuracy. A sense of the progress of ideas made it easy to justify the less immediately convincing aspects of Herodotus and therefore to eliminate any reason for preserving the old opposition between Herodotus and Thucydides.

If Herodotus was the naive, fresh contemplation of the past, Thucydides was the representative of a more thoughtful, experienced analysis of human destiny. My impression is that Herodotus was more easily appreciated in isolation during the eighteenth century than in the nineteenth century. In the eighteenth century he was the wise cosmopolitan. In the nineteenth century political history, especially in Germany—for reasons which we can leave aside here—became predominant again. Therefore Thucydides attracted greater attention and was considered more congenial than Herodotus. Yet Herodotus was never dismissed again as a liar or as an incompetent historian. Scholars in three centuries of Oriental and Greek studies had come to know better. At worst Herodotus was subordinated to Thucydides; at best he was put on the same footing with his old rival. The qualities which were now attributed to Thucydides and had first been found in Herodotus were the qualities of philosophic understanding and artistic insight. The new position of Herodotus indicated that trustworthy history need no longer be contemporary history. It indicated also that the history of civilisation—as opposed to mere political history—had come into its own. The varying fortunes of Herodotus in the eighteenth and nineteenth centuries are a symptom of the tension existing between the supporters of political history and the supporters of the history of civilisation. But even in the time and in the country of Treitschke, history of civilisation was not forgotten.

The situation was affected by many other factors. One, of a purely historiographical nature, we shall have to examine in the next chapter—namely, the intervention of the antiquarians. Research in archives and excavations, study of inscriptions and coins, made it clear that there was no substantial difference in reliability between the study of recent and the study of remote events. Thus the scope for research in extrapolitical events was enlarged. The world of Herodotus—extending over the centuries and over the various aspects of human activities in different countries—and the world of Thucydides—concentrated in one period, one country, one activity—could no longer look like two worlds apart. There is no need to add that today Herodotus is perhaps more generally appreciated, certainly more generally loved, than Thucydides. The need for a comprehensive, extrapolitical history is admitted by almost everyone. Herodotus seems to us so much more human than Thucydides. Perhaps he also offers an escape—a delightful one—from the iron tower in which Thucydides wants to shut us, after having shut himself in it. These are considerations we may take for granted. What is characteristic of the present situation is that the two rivals of Antiquity—Herodotus and Thucydides—have become the acknowledged joint founders of historical research. Herodotus would not have minded, but Thucydides must be horrified at the association.

CHAPTER THREE

The Rise of Antiquarian Research

I

Throughout my life I have been fascinated by a type of man so near to my profession, so transparently sincere in his vocation, so understandable in his enthusiasms, and yet so deeply mysterious in his ultimate aims: the type of man who is interested in historical facts without being interested in history. Nowadays the pure antiquarian is rarely met with. To find him one must go into the provinces of Italy or France and be prepared to listen to lengthy explanations by old men in uncomfortably cold, dark rooms. As soon as the antiquarian leaves his shabby palace which preserves something of the eighteenth century and enters modern life, he becomes the great collector, he is bound to specialise, and he may well end up as the founder of an institute of fine arts or of comparative anthropology. The time-honoured antiquarian has fallen victim to an age of specialisation. He is now worse than outdated: he has himself become a historical problem to be studied against the background of crosscurrents of thought and of changing "Weltanschauungen"—the very things he wanted to avoid.

Let us consider for a moment that archetype of all antiquarians: Nicolas-Claude Fabri sieur de Peiresc. He was born in 1580, and where could he have been born but in Provence, not far from Aix? He was a descendant of magistrates and members of parliament, to become himself a magistrate and member of parliament and, incidentally, a very shrewd administrator of his family estate. He remained a bachelor; and he was an inveterate traveller, far more so than his shaky health and his duties should have allowed. Aix was his love and pride, and there he died in 1637 among his collections of medals, books, plants, minerals, scientific instruments, and what not. His death was lamented in forty different languages, including Scottish, in a memorial book, a "generis humani lessus," a "complaint of the human race" called *Panglossia* compiled by the Academy of Humoristi in Rome under the patronage of Cardinal Francesco Barberini, a nephew of Pope Urban VIII. Claude de Peiresc published almost nothing: there is in print only a pamphlet on a second-rate antiquarian subject. But he wrote learned and witty letters to many of the great men of his time, from Grotius to Rubens: there are thousands of them in the Bibliothèque Méjanes of his Aix, in the Bibliothèque Inguimbertine of Carpentras and in other libraries, which have been only partially published in the monumental edition by Tamizey de Larroque and elsewhere; and in the last period of his life at least he kept a very careful register of all his correspondence. He shared in the astronomic observations of his friend Gassendi, who was to become his biographer. He experimented in physiology and performed dissections both on animals and on human bodies. Angora cats were his speciality, and he used to give them to men whom he wanted to induce to sell antiquities. He wrote to one of his agents: "If it were useful to promise one of the kittens in order to get the vase of Vivot, do not hesitate to commit yourself." For ultimately his overriding preference was for antiques—coins, statues, and manuscripts. There were seventeen thousand pieces in his *cabinet de médailles* when he died. He studied what he collected—and a great deal more besides. His name is best known in connection with the Grand Camée de Paris and with the Calendar of Philocalus: the latter, but not the former, was in his possession. Jews and heretics were among his correspondents: the two Nostradamus, Rabbi Salomon Azubius, and Tommaso Campanella. The Samaritan Bible and the Provençal troubadours were among the subjects in which he was interested.

Can we find a sense in all these chaotic activities? They certainly made sense to Peiresc's contemporaries, to begin with his biographer, P. Gassendi (1641). The name of Gassendi immediately introduces us to the circle of *libertins érudits*—Dupuy, Naudé, Gui Patin, La Mothe Le Vayer. Sextus Empiricus (translated by Henricus Stephanus into

Latin in 1562 and available in Greek since 1621) was one of their mentors. Sextus also appealed to Montaigne, who had a Jewish mother, and to Francisco Sanches, the son of Marranos, who wrote *Quod nihil scitur*. He obviously had something to offer to men living in the borderland between different religions, but he also opened up new vistas to those who were tired of theological controversies within their own confession. It is true that Peiresc does not appear to have taken part in the *débauches pyrrhoniennes* of Naudé, Gassendi, and Patin, of which Patin wrote in a famous letter (*Lettres* III, 508 of 1648). When confronted by the *Dialogues d'Oratius Tubero*—the Sceptic publication of François de La Mothe Le Vayer—Peiresc disclaimed any understanding of such deep thoughts: "moy qui ne cognoys rien en toutes ces grandes élévations d'esprit" (IV, 385). But three days later he made to his friend Gassendi one of his most forceful statements against those centuries "de grande simplicité" in which one believed everything "sans aultre preuve que de simples conjectures de ce qui pouvoit avoir esté" (IV, 383). Peiresc was a Pyrrhonist in so far as Pyrrhonists liked tangible things, and Peiresc and Gassendi agreed that empirical observation was far more trustworthy than dogmatic philosophy. As Peiresc wrote in one particular case to Père Anastase: "l'observation directe s'impose, et marque les erreurs des calculs les plus savants." His biographer in more solemn Latin confirms that Peiresc regretted the habit of overlooking what hits the eye.

It is an unrealistic question to ask whether Gassendi or Peiresc believed in Christianity. They never admitted to being unbelievers, and there is no cogent reason to assume that they were. But they turned to experiments, documents, individual facts, in a spirit of universal curiosity and distrust of dogmatism. They admired Galileo, and Peiresc with all his caution wrote to Cardinal Barberini that in condemning Galileo the Church was running the risk of appearing to posterity as the persecutor of another Socrates: "pourrait même être un jour comparée à la persécution que Socrate éprouva dans sa patrie." Galileo is a name to be retained in connection with the antiquarians. The Italian antiquarians of the seventeenth and early eighteenth centuries were quite explicit in declaring themselves his pupils. I have no doubt either that Gassendi and Peiresc and their friends were also trying to apply the Galilean method of observation to their own antiquarian studies. They were convinced that they could examine material objects of the past in a positive scientific manner, and they disliked the bias of the historians who worked on evidence provided by equally biased predecessors. We can understand why Henricus Stephanus—neither a real Catholic nor a real Calvinist—was an admirer both of Herodotus and of Sextus Empiricus: he liked Herodotus as a true collector of facts from direct observation, and in his colourful language he described Sextus Empiricus as a thinker who would help to drive to madness the dogmatic impious philosophers of modern times, "ut nostri saeculi dogmaticos impios philosophos ad insaniam redigam." Post-Herodotean historians were traditionally too much committed to political and religious controversies to be in tune with the desire for objectivity, experiment, and theological neutrality characteristic of the *érudits*.

The new Pyrrhonism turned against the reliability of ordinary historians. The antiquarians were in a stronger position. Material objects spoke for the times in which they had been made. As the great Spaniard Antonio Agustín had written in a work published in 1587, and many others had repeated later, nothing could be more reliable than Roman coins—official documents guaranteed by the Roman authorities themselves. Of course the *libertins érudits* were aware that objects can be forged, but they also knew how to detect forgeries. For one coin that is forged, a hundred are authentic and serve as a check. But how could one check the account of a battle in Thucydides or Livy if it was unique?

II

Thus Peiresc and his company provide us with at least something of an introduction to the mentality of the antiquarians. Their passion for ancient objects was the consequence of their interest in empirical observation and experiment in all fields. They distrusted literary tradition, disliked theological controversy, and had little use for ordinary political history. A fair dose of scepticism directly handed down from Sextus Empiricus contributed to their attitude. It is noteworthy that many of the great antiquarians of the seventeenth century from Charles Patin to Jacob Spon were physicians: a fact already commented upon by contemporaries. Interpretation of individual objects or inscriptions was the favourite exercise of these men. They were capable of appraising unrelated facts which to us seem entirely remote from any serious pursuit. Angelo Fabroni, who wrote the lives of some of the most important antiquarians of the seventeenth century and of his own time, emphasised with admiration the variety of subjects studied by his heroes. He never considered it necessary to find a unifying interest in them. In describing, for instance, the activities of Filippo Buonarroti he made no attempt to understand why Buonarroti had to jump from Silander and Aureliopolis "pene incognitae urbes" to the "status civitatis" of Tarsus and to the meaning of "Neocori." Indeed Buonarroti himself would never have expected his biographer to worry about that. The antiquarians loved disparate and obscure facts. But behind the individual, seemingly unrelated items there was Antiquity, mysterious and august. Implicitly every antiquarian knew that he was supposed to add to the picture of Antiquity. In practice that meant that the individual facts were collected and set aside with a view to a future general survey of those institutions, customs, cults, for which coins and inscriptions were regarded as the most important evidence. The antiquarian's mind truly wandered to and fro between single facts and general surveys. The survey, if it ever came (not very often), would never be an ordinary book of history. Antiquity was static: it called for systematic descriptions of ancient institutions, religion, law, finances. The literary form of the handbook of antiquities had been firmly established since 1583, when J. Rossfeld, called Rosinus, published his *Romanarum antiquitatum libri decem*. Later antiquarian works preserved the structure of Rosinus' book with remarkable uniformity.

The antiquarians of the seventeenth and eighteenth centuries would not have been what they were if they had considered themselves a new sect. Rather, they prided themselves on being a relic of Antiquity. The very name they used, *antiquarius*, recalled the *Antiquitates (humanae et divinae)* by Varro. They delighted in Pliny, Athenaeus, Aulus Gellius, Philostratus, and Pausanias as their predecessors. We must accept their claim to be the continuators of the ancient antiquarians.

What may seem coincidence is perhaps not entirely casual. First, in Antiquity, too, erudite research had flourished during periods of intellectual doubt. The rise of the Sophists, the birth of the great philosophic schools after Alexander, the introduction of academic scepticism in Rome in the second and first centuries B.C., are simultaneous with the best periods of ancient erudition. Second, there is a clear analogy between the systematic handbooks of the late Renaissance and the systematic organisation of ancient erudition. The systematic attitude of mind of the ancient antiquarians would appear to have been passed on to the modern ones. Third and finally, the separation of political history from antiquarian studies is also to be found in Antiquity. It happened in fact when Thucydides created political history in the age of the Sophists. It is a fair assumption that if Herodotus had remained the model historian there would never have been any antiquarians. His curiosity potentially embraced all the subjects which later became part of the antiquarian province. Thucydides saw to it that Herodotus should not prevail. In consequence history became a narration of political and military events, preference being given to the events of which the writer had been a witness. All the "classic" historians after Herodotus—Thucydides, Xenophon, Ephorus, Polybius, Sallust, Livy, Tacitus—conformed to this pattern.

Erudition, as is made clear by Polybius in his polemics against Timaeus, was not an essential, indeed not even a desirable, quality in a historian. Authors of local history, chronography, genealogy, erudite dissertations, ethnographical works, whatever their merits, did not rank as true historians. It is enough to remind ourselves that the list of the important historians in Quintilian includes, among the Greeks, Herodotus, Thucydides, Xenophon, Theopompus, Ephorus, Philistus, Clitarchus, and Timagenes. Not one antiquarian is included—nor indeed any of the historians of Attica. If the historians of Sicily are considered real historians (as the mention of Philistus shows), it is because Sicily was a world in itself, and the conflicts between Greeks and Carthaginians were of general political importance. The historians of Sicily were more than local historians. It is no accident that Antiochus of Syracuse was a source of Thucydides, whereas Philistus, next in time and in importance, was an admirer and imitator of Thucydides. No writer on religious rites, barbarian laws, obsolete names, or local history has come down to us with a reputation comparable to that of Ephorus or Sallust. Everyone sensed that writers of this kind were something other than historians. Yet there would have been no clear answer to the question as to what they actually were.

A comprehensive word to indicate what we call antiquarian studies did not exist in Antiquity, though in Hellenistic and Roman times the notion was expressed, with a certain vagueness, by terms such as κριτικός, φιλόλογος, πολυίστωρ, γραμματικός, *doctus, eruditus, literatus*. The nearest approximation was the word ἀρχαιολόγος, as it appeared in Plato. The Sophist Hippias is made to say in the Platonic *Hippias major* 285 D that genealogies of heroes and men, traditions about the foundation of cities, and lists of eponymous magistrates are part of a science called archaeology. The fact that Plato puts the word "archaeology" into the mouth of Hippias does not strictly prove that Hippias used it. But Hippias was an authority on the subjects mentioned by Plato. He compiled the list of the winners of the Olympic games, and did research on names and laws. Furthermore, archaeology is one of those abstract words which the Sophists were apt to invent. What Plato proves in any case is that either in the fifth or in the fourth century certain types of historical studies were called archaeology, not history. This convenient terminology was not generally used after the fourth century B.C. Archaeology was used in Hellenistic and Roman times to indicate a work on archaic history or a history from the origins. Dionysius of Halicarnassus' *Roman Archaeology* is an archaic history of Rome. Flavius Josephus' *Jewish Archaeology* is a history of the Jews from their origins to Josephus' own times. A work by King Juba, who wrote in the age of Augustus, could be called either Roman History or Roman Archaeology. A poem by or attributed to Semonides on the origins of Samos was retrospectively given the name of *Archaeology of Samos*, and even the *Atthis* of Phanodemus, a work of the fourth century B.C., was later called *Archaeology* because it dealt mainly with the archaic history of Athens. Thus in the Hellenistic age the word "archaeology" lost the meaning we find in Plato. If Hippias tried to establish ἀρχαιολογία as opposed to ἱστορία he failed. The other terms we mentioned, from φιλόλογος to *eruditus*, were never so precise. The failure is significant. It means that the ancients were not able to make a clear-cut distinction between proper history and a different type of research which is concerned with the past without being history.

But the failure to create a clear and permanent terminological distinction between history and the other type of research does not imply that the distinction was forgotten or felt only vaguely. Local history, genealogy, chronology, mythography, study of ancient laws, ceremonies, names, etc., developed outside the main stream of historiography. Negatively these studies were characterised by a lack of prominent political interests, by indifference to contemporary issues of general importance, and by a lack of rhetorical accomplishments. Positively they were characterised by an interest in the minute details of the past, by undisguised local patriotism, by curiosity for unusual events and monstrosities, and by display of learning as an end in itself.

One feature, not of all, but of many of these works must be underlined particularly because it was bound to determine the future of what we call antiquarian studies. It is their systematic treatment. Ordinary history is chronologically ordered. The whole sense of the historical narration depends on the time factor, on the correct succession of events. Much of the research we are now examining was not true to this chronological principle of organisation. It was systematic and covered the whole subject section by section: it was descriptive in a systematic form, not explanatory in a chronological order. This was not unnatural. If you study the names of nations, ἐθνῶν ὀνομασίαι, or the sacrifices customary in Sparta, περὶ τῶν ἐν Λακεδαίμονι θυσιῶν, the easiest approach is to examine them one by one. The dates of many political events are known, but the dates of origin of institutions and words are either unknown or difficult to discover. When chronology was easy to establish—or was the purpose of their research—the antiquarians had of course no objection to chronological order. The clearest way of writing on an antiquarian subject such as local history was to do so chronologically. Indeed in some local histories the names of the eponymous magistrates of the year were placed before the report on the events of that year. The local chronicle of Athens was organised according to the sequence of the Athenian archons (Jacoby, *Fr. Gr.*

Hist. III, b, II, p. 14, n. 132); the chronicle of Samos according to the Samian magistrates (Herod. III, 59, 4; Thucyd. I, 13, 2).

The systematic order ultimately came to represent a major, if not the only, criterion of distinction between proper history and other research about the past. Having been adopted by Varro in his *Antiquitates*, it also became a feature of Roman studies on the past and was transmitted to the humanists of the fifteenth century. The time factor thus played a lesser part in antiquarian studies than in those of political history. In their turn the works on political history generally avoided any systematic presentation: at all events no one thought of Aristotle's *Politics* (when it became known) as a book of history.

III

There is confirmation for my thesis that the rise of erudite research coincided with the creation of political thought by Thucydides. All the evidence we have seems to point to the conclusion that books on local history, as well as studies of magistrates' lists, of religious ceremonies, of proper names, and of other monuments of historical interest, were written for the first time in the last thirty years of the fifth century B.C. No doubt lists of magistrates and registrations of local events existed long before that time, but had not been made the object of scholarly research. Ethnography and genealogy were in a different position. They existed as sciences before Thucydides. As we have seen, they conditioned the work of Herodotus and became part of his ἱστορία. But when Thucydides restricted history to political events, ethnography and genealogy were turned into erudite subjects as well.

Antiquarian research—or *archaiologia*—was of practical importance. The lists of the winners of the Olympic games prepared by Hippias and the lists of the priestesses of Hera at Argos and of the winners of the Carnaean games at Sparta compiled by Hellanicus contributed to the establishment of a better chronology in the Greek world. But the issues raised or implied by many antiquarian studies were of even greater theoretical importance. The study of the origins of the cities, the comparison between barbarian and Greek laws and customs, the search for the first inventors of arts and crafts, led to an evaluation of human civilisation. Was fire, the alphabet, the taming of the horse, the discovery of navigation, a gift of the gods or a product of human activity? If man had been the inventor, how did he reach the result? By chance? By imitation? By struggling with the gods? If it was imitation, imitation of whom and what?

Whereas historical research in the Thucydidean sense banned these problems, the Sophists liked them and passed them on to later generations of philosophers and erudites. Hippias himself wrote on the names of nations, and he and Critias produced descriptions of constitutions of various cities and regions. Hellanicus was not a Sophist, though he made distinctions of a philosophic character (Arr. *Diss.* II, 19, 1, quoted by Aulus Gellius I, 2, 10); but at least from their titles his erudite subjects seem indistinguishable from those of the Sophists: "About nations, names of nations, foundations of cities and nations, laws of the Barbarians."

An element of play and pastime was inherent in erudition from its inception. When a fifth-century B.C. writer produced a dissertation about the parents and ancestors of the warriors who went to Troy, it may be assumed—or it is at least to be hoped—that he was not fully in earnest. Erudite pleasure is always ambiguous. The erudite research of the Sophists provided the necessary material for their views on human nature and civilisation and was therefore nearer to philosophy than to any other subject. The systematic character of erudition was in tune with the systematic character of philosophy. Unfortunately we are very badly informed about the theoretical writings of the Sophists on politics, but it seems likely that they used their antiquarian research to buttress their theories about law.

The connection between philosophic research and erudition was maintained in the fourth century. Plato was uninterested in history in the Thucydidean sense but encouraged research on customs and laws, to judge from his own work on the *Laws* and from the encyclopaedic activities of his pupil Heraclides Ponticus. The third book of Plato's *Laws* is an examination of the origins of civilisations according to the principles laid down by the Sophists. What Diogenes Laertius called historical books by Heraclides, "On the Pythagoreans" and "On Discoveries," are, in fact, antiquarian researches outside the main stream of history: "discoveries" are a typical subject for systematic erudition. In the school of Isocrates, which on the whole favoured Thucydidean history, a place was left to erudition for the purpose of clarifying what civilisation, or paideia, was about: Ephorus, for instance, wrote about "discoveries," *heuremata*. But, needless to say, it was in the school of Aristotle that erudition and philosophy combined most closely. Aristotle based all his conclusions, and particularly those on politics, on extensive systematic surveys of empirical knowledge. His pupils Theophrastus and Dicaearchus developed their views on religion and civilisation on the basis of antiquarian research. A famous example is Theophrastus' survey of offerings and sacrifices to gods which is also an attack against sacrifices stained with blood. One of the notable features of Aristotelian scholarship is the combination of antiquarian research with textual criticism and editorship. We find it in Alexandria, where Theophrastus' pupil, Demetrius of Phalerum, was long active. Alexandria offered another remarkable combination: that of scholarship and poetry. As Rudolf Pfeiffer has repeatedly emphasised, the combination of love of poetry with scholarship is unusual. Alexandrian poetry in the third century B.C. and French poetry in the sixteenth century are the most obvious examples of it. Callimachus and Apollonius of Rhodes pursued antiquarian research according to rules that went back to Aristotle, but they pursued poetry in a manner that—to judge by the polemics between Callimachus and the Peripatetic Praxiphanes—did not always have the approval of Aristotle's disciples.

Thucydidean history declined in the third century B.C. A few honest men, such as Ptolemy, Aristobulus, and Hieronymus of Cardia, went against the majority of their fellow-historians when they tried to restore truth and proportion to the events of an age which was becoming legendary under the very eyes of those who lived in it. A few generations later Polybius rightly felt that during the previous century love of drama and lack of practical experience had given political history a turn for the worse. Erudition prospered where political history was in decline. Egypt produced practically no serious political historian after the first King Ptolemy, but became the centre of antiquarian research. Philosophic interest continued to support erudition. One of the most important results was the notion of *bios*, of "life," which could be applied either to the individual or to a whole nation. To write the personal story of an individual was not new. In the fifth century Ion of Chios and Stesimbrotus of Thasus had provided sketches of their contemporaries. The few extant fragments show Ion of Chios to have been a delightful raconteur. Biographies had been written in the fourth century. We have one, Xenophon's *Agesilaus*, or perhaps two, if we take Isocrates' *Euagoras* as a primitive type of biography. Biographies, however, multiplied only in the Alexandrian age, and there is hardly any doubt that the Peripatetics were largely responsible for this development. They were interested in types, and in the last analysis the study of biography was to them a study in human types. They studied tyrants, artists, poets, and philosophers in biographical form.

This is not the place to discuss the problems connected with the development of Greek biography; nor is this the moment to decide whether biography was history to the Greeks, though no ancient authority includes a biographer among the good historians. What is certain (as Friedrich Leo explained in 1901) is that in the Hellenistic and Roman periods biography was written in two forms, as either chronologically ordered biography or systematically organised biography. The latter interests us here.

The lives of politicians and generals were usually written in proper chronological sequence. We can see in Plutarch that such lives had much in common with ordinary political history of the Thucydidean type, if we disregard the fact that ordinary history of the Thucydidean type did not include many biographical details. The lives of poets, artists, and philosophers were often written in a systematic way, examining in succession the various aspects of a given personality. Diogenes Laertius provides lives of philosophers of this type; and it was one of the more speculative aspects of Leo's theory on Greek biography that when Suetonius wrote his lives of the Caesars in a systematic order he transferred to men of action a form of biography that had originally been meant for writers and artists.

The biographical form we find in Suetonius and Diogenes Laertius is certainly in keeping with Alexandrian antiquarianism, indeed it had all the characteristics we associate with antiquarian research. It must be compared with the biographical information that the librarians of Alexandria included in their tables or guides, *Pinakes*. It was also the type of biography which was not confined to the study of individual lives. Dicaearchus wrote a life of Greece, which was imitated by Varro's *Life of the Roman People* and perhaps also by another *Life of Greece* attributed to a Jason. It is true that Dicaearchus made some distinction between primitive life and civilised life, and he discussed at length the distinctive features of primitive life, which he was inclined to see through rose-coloured glasses. But when he came to more recent times, he seems to have paid little attention to chronological order and to have proceeded to a systematic description of Greek customs and institutions in the Suetonian manner. A curious by-product of this systematic and erudite biography is the work by Varro, *Imagines* or *Hebdomades*, in which seven hundred portraits of Romans and non-Romans were collected, each with his own eulogy.

Historical research in its antiquarian form was also distinguished by the extensive use of charters, inscriptions, and monuments. Serious historians from Thucydides to Polybius, from Fabius Pictor to Tacitus, occasionally availed themselves of archives, but not one of them ever began writing a history by a systematic search of the documents. Not even Dionysius of Halicarnassus, who was under the influence of Varro, thought it necessary to make a thorough study of the material in Roman archives. Historians seldom went to archives, and even more rarely did they quote *in extenso* the documents they happened to have found there. Erudites, φιλόλογοι, made it their business to assemble documents. Aristotle's work on the dramatic performances in Athens was founded upon the original records. Craterus, perhaps his younger contemporary, copied and published Attic decrees (Jacoby, *Fr. Gr. Hist.*, no. 342). Polemon wrote a work "on inscriptions city by city," and we know that at least in one case he quoted an Attic decree literally (C. Müller, *Fragm. Hist. Graec.* III, 138). The work of Hellenistic chronologists is founded upon the exploration of public records—such as lists of magistrates (for which Hippias had provided the example in the fifth century). Later Varro used official documents in support of his etymologies. He delved into *censoriae tabulae, commentarii consulares, libri augurum, carmina saliorum*, and so forth.

Statues, temples, votive objects, were illustrated in monographs and general handbooks. Herodotus, of course, had examined with care the monuments he saw. But Thucydidean historiography was sparing in its use of evidence from monuments; and after Thucydides the study of archaeological and epigraphical evidence was never again part of the business of the ordinary historian. By way of compensation the old type of geographical description, the *periegesis*, was transformed to satisfy the needs of antiquarian research on monuments. The geographer often became an antiquarian. In the second century B.C., Polemon probably called himself a *periegetes*: he was in fact a learned guide, the remote predecessor of Burckhardt's *Cicerone*. The antiquarian monograph could be so narrow as to include only the monuments of the Athenian acropolis or so wide as to embrace the whole of Greece— which is what Pausanias almost did. Polemon went even beyond Greece and wrote on Samothrace and Carthage. Local histories became full of antiquarian details, and the greatest of the local historians of Athens, Philochorus, was also one of the most active writers of monographs on Attic inscriptions, religious institutions, and other antiquarian subjects. We may take these monographs as the by-products of his *Atthis*.

IV

To sum up what I cannot here discuss in detail, we can see five main lines in Hellenistic erudition. One is the editing of and commenting on literary texts. The second is the collection of early traditions about individual cities, regions, sanctuaries, gods, and institutions. The third is the systematic description of monuments and copying of inscriptions. The fourth is the compilation of learned biographies, and the fifth is chronology. None of these types of research was absolutely new in the Hellenistic age, and none was invariably treated in a systematic way. Some of the subjects which we should nowadays put into the centre of historical research were left to the erudite scholars. They dealt with the original evidence about the past, they studied the earliest manifestations of civilisation, they kept closely in touch with philosophy, and indeed they were the professional biographers. Political historians took cognizance of these subjects only marginally and therefore were unable to present history in a wider context. On the other hand the erudites seldom tried to connect their subjects with political developments.

I should not care to be asked for a simple judgement on the difference between the erudition of the third century B.C. and the erudition of the succeeding two centuries. Clearly the continuity in themes and methods was somehow affected by the general decline in the Hellenistic world in the second and first centuries B.C. under the pressure of the Romans. Bigger factors than mere intellectual limitations and mistakes explain the obvious lack of creativeness which one notices in large sectors of the historiography and the erudition of the second and especially of the first century B.C. In particular the historical studies of the first century B.C. are more conspicuous for their encyclopaedic character, both on the political and on the erudite side, than for their originality of ideas: Alexander Polyhistor, Castor, Trogus Pompeius, Diodorus, were comprehensive, not creative, writers. Yet Roman imperialism was not an entirely negative influence. Polybius and Posidonius are unthinkable without Rome, even as the wide horizons of the Roman *orbis* account in some measure for the wide range of Alexander Polyhistor, Trogus Pompeius, and Diodorus. Polybius recognised that the Romans had made universal history possible. Furthermore, the Romans themselves discovered a source of national strength in erudition. They brought to the task of assimilating the methods of Greek scholarship a sense of urgency that must have surprised their Greek masters. Historical erudition came closer to politics in Rome than in the Hellenistic world. Antiquarian research revealed to the Romans customs to be revived and precedents to be used. Emperors like Augustus and Claudius were quick to grasp the advantages inherent in a well-exploited antiquarianism.

Varro inherited the *esprit de système* of his Hellenistic forbears, but applied it with a consistency, a strength, and a fullness of results that overshadowed all his predecessors. His contemporaries were astounded, and five centuries later St. Augustine was still under his spell. Twenty-five books dealt with the *antiquitates rerum humanarum*, and sixteen with the *antiquitates rerum divinarum*: the very parallelism of the two series is something unknown to the Greeks. Varro liked to alternate systematic works with observations on miscellaneous subjects. His successors, from Suetonius to John Lydus in the sixth century, followed him in both directions.

Antiquarian learning remained a living inspiration in Rome to the end: it is enough to mention the antiquarian erudition of the so-called last pagans in the fourth century A.D., Servius, Macrobius, Symmachus. But there was never another Varro. That is, there was never again a situation in which the discovery of new facts was pursued so relentlessly and effectively as in the time of Caesar. In Rome, perhaps even more quickly than in the Hellenistic kingdoms, erudition became compilation, and compilation led to summaries, excerpts, scholia—the end of vigorous creative research. Consequently the trend towards fusion of antiquarian and historical research became insignificant after Augustus. A historian with antiquarian interests like Dionysius of Halicarnassus remained an exception. Later Tacitus could derive good marginal effects from antiquarian details, but nothing more. The antiquarians, indeed, kept up their traditional link with the philosophers: from Varro to Macrobius many of them were interested in philosophy, but none seems to have been an original thinker. It is significant that antiquarian research was made to contribute to religious polemics both on the pagan and on the Christian side. But perhaps the only Roman philosopher who used antiquarian research to establish new philosophic propositions was St. Augustine: and the new propositions were such as to render further antiquarian research superfluous.

Research on antiquities did not suffer total interruption in the Western Middle Ages, to which I should like to confine my remarks. Encyclopaedias (such as that by Isidore of Seville) transmitted general notions about classical antiquity. The systematic description of institutions and customs did not disappear altogether. The ruins of Rome were the subject of constant curiosity, and the descriptions of such antiquities—the *Mirabilia*—are specimens of a systematic survey. Inscriptions were collected occasionally; individual monuments or gems were examined. Ecclesiastical historians used inscriptions and other antiquarian evidence to establish their claims. In the ninth century Agnellus of Ravenna is a specially notable example with his *Liber Pontificalis*. William of Malmesbury's *De antiquitate Glastoniensis Eccle-*

siae is a later and better-known work of the same genre. But both quantitatively and qualitatively this type of research was too restricted to be of real consequence for historical studies. The cultivation of systematic antiquarian research was in abeyance from the middle of the seventh century to the fourteenth century.

A few facts stand out. In the fourteenth century Petrarch examined ancient literary sources with a care for details of language and history that had not been equalled since the fourth century A.D. He used Roman coins to correct or supplement literary evidence. His friend Giovanni Dondi made a detailed study of monuments with a scientific technique such as no ancient antiquarian had ever used. In the matter of Roman topography, as in many other subjects, Petrarch was heavily indebted to the mediaeval tradition: the *Mirabilia* were still authoritative for him. But he had found a new method which in the course of the next two generations was bound to bring about a complete break with *Mirabilia* and mediaeval encyclopaedias.

Boccaccio's *Genealogia Deorum* and Salutati's *De laboribus Herculis* still show an obvious dependence on mediaeval methods of interpretation. Biondo's *Roma Triumphans* and Politian's *Miscellanea* belong to a new and different world—they develop Petrarch's method to its full potentialities. Politian's case is the simpler. He imitated in the *Miscellanea* the combination of antiquarian and philological research which Aulus Gellius had displayed in the *Noctes Atticae*. The main difference is that he was so much more accurate and intelligent than Aulus Gellius. Biondo revived ancient forms that had disappeared a thousand years before. He deliberately tried to revive Varro's *Antiquitates*. The result, which was perhaps somewhat different from the original Varro, became the prototype of all later antiquarian research on ancient Rome. After having devoted his *Roma Triumphans* to Roman institutions and *Roma Instaurata* to Roman topography, he produced his most original work in the *Italia Illustrata*. Others followed Biondo with similar researches on Germany, Spain, and Britain. Biondo rigorously separated antiquarian research from history, though he was also interested in the latter and was indeed one of the founders of mediaeval history with his *Historiae ab inclinatione Romanorum*. Just as Politian was the master of the new research on individual details,

Biondo was the forerunner of the systematic antiquarian handbooks, the founder of modern scientific research on the antiquities of all the countries of Europe.

V

The infamous word "Renaissance" has a precise meaning when applied to the historical research of the fifteenth and sixteenth centuries. Something really was called back to life: the ancient erudite research as a discipline of its own, not to be confused with history. In the fifteenth century the term "antiquarius" acquired the meaning of "student of ancient objects, customs, institutions, with a view to reconstructing ancient life." Felice Feliciano called himself "antiquarius" in that classic text of fifteenth-century antiquarianism, the *Iubilatio*. Philology and antiquarianism had been inseparable in antiquity; they were again inseparable in the Renaissance. It is more difficult to decide to what extent the old link between philosophy and antiquarianism was renewed in the fifteenth and sixteenth centuries. The antiquarians normally brought strong religious, artistic, and political views to bear on their work. There were antiquarians who liked paganism (such as Pomponio Leto). Others (such as Guillaume Budé) were concerned with the relations between Hellenism and Christianity. The majority looked upon Antiquity as a model for art, architecture, and festivals, and admired Roman law and institutions. Antiquarianism appealed as a revival of ancient forms of life: it helped nations to self-confidence by rediscovering their ancient traditions. The emulators of Biondo in Germany, Spain, and Britain contributed to the formation of nationalism in their respective countries.

Theorists of history at first ignored antiquarian research altogether and later declared it history of a different and less perfect class. In 1605, after having distinguished between Antiquities, Memorials, and Perfect History, Francis Bacon called antiquities "history defaced or some remnants of history which have casually escaped the shipwreck of time." The distinction was echoed by Gerard J. Vossius in his threefold division of *antiquitates, memoriae, et historia iusta*. The Thucydidean or Livian type of history—the narration in chronological order of political and military events—was held in higher esteem than the antiquarian effort to reconstruct institutions and customs systematically.

Hybrids combining historical narration with systematic research did exist, but to the best of my knowledge these were not concerned with Rome or Greece as a whole. They were to be found in works of ethnography and local history. We have seen that in Greece, too, ancient ethnography and local history had more affinity with antiquarian than with historical works. Tommaso Fazello's *De rebus siculis* (1558) can provide an example. The first part of the work is arranged, not chronologically, but geographically as a survey of the cities of the island. The second part is a history of Sicily.

While the philosophic and theological implications of antiquarian research were often vague in the fifteenth and sixteenth centuries, they became much more definite in the following century. As I have mentioned in connection with Peiresc, the antiquarians thought that they were applying Galileo's method to the study of the past. Two generations after Peiresc, Giovanni Giusto Ciampini made antiquarian research a part of the activities of his Roman *Accademia fisico-matematica*. In the seventeenth century political and religious controversies had an adverse effect on ordinary historical studies. Pyrrhonists were asking loudly whether historical books could be considered more than partisan views of events. Ordinary historians faced discredit for their services to dynastic and sectarian causes. But the antiquarians were not involved in this discredit. They maintained the attitude of uncommitted scholars. They felt that they belonged to an international brotherhood. Religious and political differences represented no barriers for them. Their answer to the doubts about the reliability of history was to point to evidence of undisputed authenticity—coins, statues, buildings, inscriptions. The Pyrrhonist F. W. Bierlingius went so far as to insinuate that even coins were subject to contrasting interpretations, and G.-Ch. Le Gendre admitted that "marble and bronze sometimes lie." But Addison replied that "it is much safer to quote a medal than an author." And Charles Patin added that by their objectivity ancient coins help the historian to control his passions.

It would be naive to accept the antiquarians' claims of impartiality at their face value. The antiquarians did in fact use more literary evidence than they cared to admit, and they were more involved in religious and dynastic policies than they should have been to preserve their impartiality. Antiquarian books devoted to the relations between Paganism, Judaism, and Christianity became fashionable. They were written by *érudits* in full command of all the relative evidence; and what strange books they often were: the authors, such as Athanasius Kircher, combined learning with all sorts of theological views. Another common type of antiquarian book was that in support of dynastic or ecclesiastic claims to ancient origins or privileges: the political battles between princes and those between ecclesiastical seats were often fought by antiquarians with antiquarian weapons. Jesuits and Benedictines notoriously tried to undermine each other's ground by discovering forgeries in the opposite camp. It remains true, however, that the introduction of antiquarian arguments represented a definite improvement in ecclesiastic and dynastic controversies. Sophistry and invectives were discouraged as being of no avail against a methodical use of inscriptions and archival documents. When Mabillon, to refute Papebrochius, produced his *De re diplomatica*, Papebrochius was the first to congratulate his opponent. The Carmelites, who did not respect the rules of the game and had Papebrochius condemned by the Spanish Inquisition (1695) because of his doubts about the antiquity of their Order, were discredited in all learned circles.

VI

If a distinction has to be made between religious persuasions in the field of antiquarian studies in the seventeenth century, I would suggest that the Catholics came to rely rather more than the Protestants on inscriptions and coins and archaeological evidence. The Protestants had used Bible criticism and the study of the Fathers to buttress their position. The initiative in the criticism of literary texts was theirs. Richard Simon deluded himself when he thought that he could carry Bible criticism into the Catholic camp: Bossuet, with an eye to Spinoza, decided that his attempt should be exposed and punished. Monuments, inscriptions, relics, and liturgy were a new area in which the Catholics had good reason to trust themselves. They had the advantage of controlling Rome, with its wealth of pagan and Christian documents. They also sensed, quite rightly, that archaeology was likely to bear out many, if not all, traditions. Furthermore, under Protestant pressure the Catholics felt the need to eliminate late accretions to their cult—and here again antiquarian research could help. Rome became a centre of antiquarian research on early Christianity; and in 1632 A. Bosio's *Roma sotterranea*, the first classic study of Christian Rome, appeared. Raffaello Fabretti, the founder of modern epigraphical methods, and Ciampini worked in Rome in official capacities. In France the Benedictines of St. Maur increasingly monopolised antiquarian studies.

The achievements of the antiquarians of the seventeenth century could not fail to attract the attention of the ordinary historians. About 1715, in his projects for a reform of the Universities of Padua and Turin, Scipione Maffei indicated the necessity of introducing the study of inscriptions, coins, and charters as part of the historian's training. Later in the century A. L. von Schlözer and J. C. Gatterer made Göttingen the centre of a historical school in which the antiquarian's work was officially recognised as ancillary to historical research.

In other places historians were slower. The use of inscriptions, coins, and charters for ordinary historical research was far from being common in the late eighteenth and early nineteenth century. After all even as late as about 1850 Grote's *History of Greece* was written mainly on literary evidence: inscriptions counted for little, archaeological remains for even less. Neither Grote nor Boeckh nor Burckhardt ever saw Greece. Moreover, the use of nonliterary evidence in historical research did not necessarily mean that the ordinary historians were ready to shoulder the specific problems dealt with by the antiquarians. Many historians who used nonliterary evidence remained interested in political and military history rather than in institutions and in cultural history. The form of their historical books continued to be the chronologically organised "story," while the antiquarians remained faithful to their systematic handbooks and to their miscellaneous dissertations.

There were further complications in the situation. Though the antiquarians had gained the respect of many historians by the soundness of their use of nonliterary evidence, they had also made new and dangerous enemies. They were no longer able to rely on the traditional alliance with the philosophers. The French Encyclopaedists declared war upon erudition and carried the day. Gibbon noticed what had happened: "In France . . . the learning and language of Greece were neglected by a philosophic age." It is not possible to analyse here the reasons for the Encyclopaedists' hostility to erudition. At any rate they realised that erudition had ceased to be an ally of freedom of thought, as it had been in the days of Bayle. The alliance was severed as a result of the remarkable revival of Catholic scholarship in France and Italy between 1690 and 1740. After Mabillon, Montfaucon, Tillemont, and Muratori it was clearly difficult to accuse the Catholics of being ignorant or uncritical. In learned disputes they showed as much knowledge and critical sense as their rivals. They had learned how to use footnotes, once the favourite polemical instrument of Bayle. Therefore Voltaire abolished footnotes altogether. On a higher level, the Encyclopaedists' attack against erudition turned on the meaning of history. They fully recognised the importance of the subjects studied by the antiquarians—law, political institutions, religions, customs, inventions. They thought, however, that the antiquarians studied them in the wrong way, by accumulating insignificant details and ignoring the struggle between the forces of reason and those of superstition. One of Voltaire's essential tenets in regard to history was that too many details prevent the understanding of "l'esprit des tems et les mœurs des peuples." One must admit that his attack was launched at a time when the antiquarians had become a rather conservative body.

There was, however, no cogent reason why philosophic history should not have been associated with erudition. Voltaire's hatred of the *érudits* was not the rule forever and everywhere. In Italy, Vico had somehow prepared the way for a synthesis of philosophy and erudition. In Germany and England some historians soon combined the two elements. Winckelmann's *History of Greek Art* and Gibbon's *Decline and Fall* are the products of this combination, and we know how conscious Gibbon was of being both an antiquary and a philosopher— that is, he was a philosophic historian with the antiquarian's love of minutiae and nonliterary evidence.

If a survey had been made of historical studies a few years before the French Revolution, it would probably have disclosed the following situation. The methods of antiquarian research were slowly gaining ground in political history, but the philosophic historians were still trying to discover the course of civilisation with only a minimum of erudite research. The antiquarians themselves were doing their work with the uneasy feeling, betrayed in their prefaces, of being old-fashioned. Only a few philosophic historians had boldly decided to combine philosophy with antiquarianism; and the results fully justified their attempts.

In the course of the nineteenth century Winckelmann and Gibbon became the acknowledged masters: the two types of historical research increasingly acted upon each other and came near to synthesis. Mommsen built his Roman history on legal texts, inscriptions, coins, and study of old Italic languages. He did pioneer work of lasting importance in all these fields, while firmly aiming at political history. In Germany especially, several theorists of historiography denied antiquities the right to survive as an independent subject. F. Ritschl, the great Latin scholar, expressed his views in 1833; and thirty years later J. G. Droysen simply omitted to give a place to antiquarian studies in his theory of historical method. What matters more, the old systematic treatises about the four antiquities were gradually replaced by ordinary historical expositions. K. O. Müller wrote a history of Greek mythology instead of a handbook of religious antiquities. L. Friedländer replaced by his celebrated *Sittengeschichte* the ordinary Private Antiquities of the Romans. H. Köchly and others wrote histories of the ancient art of war instead of treatises on military antiquities. The perfect fusion of antiquarian research and Thucydidean history might have seemed only a question of time. But somehow the fusion was never perfectly achieved. Something stood in its path.

Mommsen, for instance, was adamant. He wrote his *Staatsrecht* and *Strafrecht* in a systematic way and never condescended to become a historian of Roman institutions. He insisted on the theoretical soundness of his method: individual institutions are part of a whole and must be studied as such; this is the way to avoid Niebuhr's fancies about archaic Rome. In case anyone is inclined to suspect Mommsen of merely reactionary views in the matter of historical method, I hasten to add that Burckhardt, in writing both his study of the Italian Renaissance and his history of Greek civilisation, used the descriptive and systematic method of the antiquarians rather than the rigorous chronological order of the true historians. The theologians for their part never abandoned the systematic for the chronological study of Judaism and Christianity (and were therefore often accused of being unable to understand history). Even at the beginning of this century Eduard Meyer did not hesitate to accept the distinction between history and antiquities.

Superficially the distinction was indefensible. Institutions and religious customs are clearly the result of evolution and can be treated historically only in chronological order. Mommsen's way of taking the Roman state as a Platonic idea and of analysing it in its constituent parts cannot stand up to criticism: one of his pupils, E. Täubler, pointed this out in no uncertain terms.

In the attitude of Mommsen and those who shared his beliefs there was no doubt a considerable element of intellectual conservatism. Scholars who have received a juridical or theological education are notorious both for their love of systematic treatises and for their unwillingness to seek historical explanations. Moreover, German nineteenth-century historiography as a whole reacted against the eighteenth-century idea that the history of civilisation is more important than political history. If the typical historians of the eighteenth century are students of civilisation—Voltaire, Condorcet, Ferguson, Robertson—the great names in German historiography of the nineteenth century, from Droysen to Treitschke, are mainly political historians. This statement could be qualified in a hundred ways, but generally speaking it holds good and also explains why Ranke insisted on giving priority to foreign policy, that is, to undiluted political history. The situation, at least in Germany, was favourable to the continued separation between political history and antiquarian research on nonpolitical subjects, such as law and religion.

Yet we can now say with hindsight that the survival of antiquarian research was something more than a phenomenon of academic conservatism. Anyone who has tried to write a history of institutions or of religion knows that it is not so easy to jettison the systematic for the chronological order. What Mommsen only implied has now become a basic tenet of sociology, anthropology, and what is more vaguely known as structuralism. Institutions are interconnected, individual laws and customs and ceremonies are explained by other laws and customs and ceremonies. Every state or nation has a system of beliefs, of institutions, of laws, of customs, which must be seen as a whole. The dilemma is here. Beliefs and institutions have a beginning, an evolution, and an end: we can and must write their history. In any case a history of religion and of law is no longer in dispute: it does exist. But no mere history has so far succeeded in conveying the inner coherence, the meaning, of a political institution or of a religion. Antiquarians were traditionally close to the philosophers because their systematic approach to institutions and beliefs allowed a critical evaluation of the principles underlying a system of law or religion. The elimination of the systematic approach in favour of the historical one would make any criticism of a philosophic nature very difficult. How are we going to understand and criticise a system of law, a religion, an institution, if the emphasis is on its transient and episodic evolution? Marvellous works such as Mommsen's *Staatsrecht* or Jhering's *Geist des römischen Rechts* were possible only because their authors preferred the permanent to the transient.

I think by now we are all aware of this dilemma, though we are not all certain of finding a way out of it. What I can add without going beyond the realm of fact is that the most common attempt to solve the dilemma in recent times has been to admit the structural study of institutions and beliefs as the necessary complement to a historical study of them. The more so because only a system of beliefs or institutions may be compared with other systems; and we are now all convinced that comparative methods help us to understand historical facts. I do not know enough about the history of sociology and anthropology to be able to say to what extent antiquarian studies contributed to the origins of modern sociology and anthropology. In some individual cases the relationship between antiquarian studies and sociology is obvious: Max Weber was, and felt himself to be, a pupil of Mommsen. Émile Durkheim was a pupil of N. Fustel de Coulanges, another forerunner of structuralism in his *Cité Antique*. In other cases the situation is not so clear. W. Roscher, the founding father of modern *Staatswis-*

senschaft, was the greatest admirer of Thucydides. Whatever the genetic relationship between antiquarian and structural study may be, it is a fact that structuralism is now taking over the systematic approach of the antiquarians. Whether that will ultimately prove to be a satisfactory solution is another matter.

With the gradual disappearance of the Thucydidean, or political, approach to history, history is no longer confined to political events. Everything is now capable of history, as, in one sense, it was when Herodotus started the business of history. In that sense antiquarianism, being the counterpart of the political approach to history, is by now dead. But the task of systematic descriptions of institutions and beliefs is not something which may easily be written off as useless. The rise of sociology is certainly connected with the decline of antiquarianism because sociology is the legitimate heir of antiquarian studies. It is clear that the three-cornered relationship between philosophy, antiquarianism, and perfect history is now being replaced by the relationship between philosophy, sociology, and history. Hippias has his successor in Comte, and the obstinate refusal of Mommsen to abandon the antiquarian approach to Roman institutions has been vindicated by his pupil Max Weber. In this sense antiquarianism is alive, and we have not yet heard the last of it.

CHAPTER FOUR

Fabius Pictor and the Origins of National History

I

So far it has been plain sailing: Greek historiography exists; the conflict between the Herodotean and the Thucydidean tradition in historiography becomes obvious as soon as you begin to think about it. So is the secular conflict between the antiquarian and the historian. I shall go back to the obvious in my last two lectures when I shall deal with the Tacitean tradition (that is, with the tradition of political history writing and political thinking deriving from Tacitus) and with the new type of historiography introduced by Christianity, namely, ecclesiastical history.

But Greek historiography is surrounded by large uncharted territories in which exploration has hardly begun. There are two zones into which I should like to make limited forays today. I want to deal briefly with the question of what the Greeks may have learned from the Persians in the matter of history writing: this will involve the Jews for reasons which will soon become apparent. I also want to define what the Romans knew about history before they met the Greeks. What unifies the two questions is of course the intermediary position of Greek culture between the East and the Roman West. But I should like this lecture also to represent an object lesson in the *ars nesciendi*, in the art of recognising the limits of our present knowledge.

The original lecture title was "Fabius Pictor and the Introduction of Greek Historiography to Rome."

The first question about possible Persian influences involves two points of Greek historiography which, in more than one sense, contradict each other: the use of documents—that supreme sign of respectability for the professional historian; and the abuse of storytelling—that sure sign of illicit traffic with fiction.

The second question about the pre-Greek stage of Latin history writing involves some very important aspects of Latin culture: how it suddenly jumped from a stage of crude annalistic writing in Latin to accomplished historical writing, first in Greek (remarkably enough) and then in Latin; and how it created the prototype of modern national history. The Greeks were never able to produce a tradition of national political history for themselves, for the simple reason that they were never politically unified. It was easier for them to write on Egypt or Babylonia as political entities than on Greece as a political entity. The Romans—not the Greeks—transmitted to the Renaissance the notion of national history. Livy was the master. Our second question therefore involves an attempt to clarify what in the Roman tradition prepared this very important and dangerous development, the creation of national history.

II

We all know what is the traditional account of the rise of national history in the Renaissance. It runs approximately like this. In conscious imitation of Livy, Leonardo Bruni wrote the history of Florence, Marcantonio Sabellico and Bembo wrote the history of Venice, Giorgio Merula wrote the history of the Visconti of Milan, and so forth. In the same way Enea Silvio Piccolomini wrote the history of Bohemia, Antonio Bonfini the history of Hungary, Lucio Marineo Siculo the history of Spain, Polydore Vergil the history of England, Paolo Emilio the history of France. Politian was asked to write the history of Portugal. Italian humanists made an honest living from hawking national history according to classical models. They sold this new brand of history to the kings of the nations and eventually roused the native historians to competition. About 1500 Jacob Wimpfeling "videns Romanas, Venetas, Anglas, Pannonumque et Bohemorum ac Francigenum historias in dies lectum iri" first encouraged a friend, then undertook himself, to write an *Epithoma rerum Germanicarum*—"ad gloriam Germanorum sempiternam." The Scots, too, unlike the Sassenachs, did not need to hire an Italian to write their national history in a Livian style. Though he started later than Polydore Vergil, Hector Boece (Boethius) completed his *Scotorum Historiae* in 1527, seven years before the *Anglica Historia* was published. He was given a pension of fifty Scottish pounds until his promotion to a benefit of one hundred marks. Of course Boece forged some of his evidence, but at least he produced good homemade forgeries, not concoctions by a mercenary "polutinge our Englyshe chronycles most shamefullye with his Romishe lyes and other Italyshe beggerye," as John Bayle said of Polydore Vergil.

There are obvious limitations in this account. The importance of Livy is real enough for the genesis of modern national histories. But the more one thinks about it, the less Livy one finds.

First of all there is a type of humanistic picture of a nation which has little to do with Livy. This is the type of which the best representative is Camden's *Britannia*. By way of an introduction Camden has conventional chapters of historical narration on pre-Roman Britain, Roman Britain, and the Anglo-Saxon and later invaders. But the bulk of his work is of course a systematic description of Britain in which each place is presented with its monuments, men, institutions, and memorable events from antiquity to Camden's own day. Besides, there are chapters on the laws and institutions of the country as a whole. The systematic character of the exposition—which anticipates certain features of modern social history—would have been even greater in the other work Camden planned and of which the so-called *Remains of Britain* gives us an idea. The prototype of Camden's *Britannia* is clearly Biondo's *Italia Illustrata*. I will pass on to Renaissance specialists the old poser: did Biondo have a model? In his *Roma Triumphans*, Biondo was inspired by Varro's *Antiquitates*—or more precisely by what St. Augustine had told him about Varro's *Antiquitates*. But I do not know of a model for the *Italia Illustrata*.

What concerns us here is that the Biondo-Camden type of systematic description of a nation not only competes with the Livian type, but is often found to be inextricably mixed with the Livian type. A limited mixture we have already found in Camden himself. But the mixture is far greater in other works in which scholars are inclined to find Livian inspiration. For instance, Marineo Siculo's *De rebus Hispaniae memorabilibus* is a combination of ordinary political history with a systematic geographical and ethnographical survey, including a reasoned list of Spanish saints. Admittedly *De rebus Hispaniae memorabilibus* puts together the preceding works by Marineo on Spain, beginning with *De Hispaniae laudibus* of about forty years before (1495). Marineo Siculo deserves further attention by Renaissance scholars, but the mixture of the Livian (annalistic) type and of the Biondo (systematic) type is beyond dispute. The same is true of Wimpfeling, though to a lesser degree.

III

This is only the first complication in our quest for origins. The other very obvious fact, only too often forgotten, is that in the late Roman Empire national histories were fashionable—mere summaries for Rome, but complex narrations when the subject was provided by the newly emerging nations. Our humanistic historians knew of course their Jordanes, Gregory of Tours, Isidore of Seville, and Bede. Besides, they used mediaeval chroniclers, who in their turn had used Late Antique models. The influence of Jordanes, Gregory of Tours, and Bede was twofold, being both direct and indirect. Polydore Vergil, to give the most trivial instance, admires and follows both Bede ("than whom he had not seen more sound, sincere and true historian") and William of Malmesbury, who in his turn made an exception for Bede in his contempt for predecessors. One particularly significant case is that of Enea Silvio Piccolomini. In his *Historia Bohemica* he used native chronicles in Latin. As I have never read them, I cannot say whether they were influenced by Late Antique models. But it is often forgotten that Enea Silvio, besides being a great student of Biondo, picked up a copy of Jordanes in a Swiss library and made a summary of it.

The Late Antique writers themselves, of course, worked within a tradition. It is enough to glance at Jordanes' summary of Cassiodorus on the Goths to realise that Cassiodorus quoted a string of ancient writers. We know the importance of Josephus' *Jewish Antiquities* for Cassiodorus from his *Institutiones*. Josephus is "paene secundus Livius" to Cassiodorus (1, 17, 15). In those Vivarium days, long after the composition of the Gothic history, Cassiodorus initiated and supervised the translation of the whole of the *Jewish Antiquities*. This gives relevance to the remark by Jordanes (*Getica* 4, 29) in which he regrets that Josephus, "annalium relator verissimus," did not report on the origins of the Goths.

As the structure of Josephus' *Jewish Antiquities* owed much to Dionysius of Halicarnassus' *Roman Antiquities*, and Dionysius in turn depended on Roman annalists, we have in a sense gone full circle and come back to the world of the Roman annalists to whom Livy belongs. But only in a sense. Josephus reminds us that there was another tradition which counted in creating mediaeval national history: the tradition which we can call sacred history, because it includes the Bible, Josephus, the Ecclesiastical History by Eusebius, Christian chronography, and the lives of saints. Neither Cassiodorus, who was a Roman, nor his epitomist Jordanes, who was probably a Goth, was ever tempted to treat the Goths as a religiously chosen nation: both were Catholic, whereas the majority of the Goths were heretics. But it is a well-recognised fact that, in different ways, Gregory of Tours, Isidore, and Bede introduce an element of ecclesiastical history into their accounts. Gregory is the most inclined to quote the Bible. We have repeatedly been assured that Bede never quotes the Bible in his history. But even so his account of the events between A.D. 410 and 597 is based on the *Vita Germani* by Constantius—a saint's life—and on that *De Excidio et conquestu Britanniae* by Gildas which is literally inspired by Jeremiah. It has also been observed that Isidore presents the kings of the Visigoths of Spain as the Lord's Anointed, as God's vicars.

IV

Though so much has been written on the Christian vision of history in the Late Antique historians, my impression is that at present we do not know enough about the various ingredients which they combined in their works. But one fact forcibly emerges from what we do know. We see the Late Antique historians turning to the historians of Rome, to the historians of the Church, and to the historians of Oriental nations—especially of the Jews—in order to build up their national histories. We do not see them turning to the historians of Greece. As is evident from my formulation, by historians of Greece I mean precisely historians of Greece, not historians writing in Greek about other nations. This fact suggests two problems: (1) Why were the Greeks left out in this intellectual operation, the creation of national history? (2) If it is true that the Greeks were virtually left out of the Late Antique national histories, is this also true of the Renaissance national histories?

I begin with the second question, about the Renaissance. I do not know enough to answer it. But I want to make one or two specific remarks which can help to focus future discussion. It would be foolish to take Polybius as a historian of the Greek world who, through Leonardo Bruni and subsequent Florentine historiography, contributed to the formation of modern national history. Bruni treated Polybius as a historian of Rome and derived from him the history of the First Punic War. On the other hand we cannot rule out a priori the influence of Xenophon's *Hellenica* on Bruni's notion of a national history: Bruni produced his *Commentaria rerum Graecarum*, a paraphrase of Xenophon, in the years in which he was finishing his *Historia Florentini populi*. For our purpose it is irrelevant to discuss whether in the Renaissance scholars made a distinction between history of a city and history of a nation. The Romans had been both a city and a nation. The Florentines were both a city and a nation. Bruni, to say the least, was entitled to turn to the Greeks.

How complex these things are can be indicated by the following two episodes, both connected with that remarkable man whose name I shall give as Damianus a Goes to save us from problems of Portuguese pronunciation. Damianus a Goes in his Louvain days wrote a pamphlet to demonstrate the wealth of Spain against the denigrations of the great geographer Sebastian Münster. It was published in 1541 with the title *Hispania*. Petrus Nannius, the professor of humanities at Louvain, commended the pamphlet with the remark that it imitated Thucydides in giving an idea of the material wealth of a nation—a thing which the Latin historians had often overlooked: "qua in re utinam aliquot Latini scriptores diligentiores essent, eaque in parte Thucydidem imitarentur." This is one of the most interesting compliments paid to Thucydides as a political historian in the sixteenth century. It presupposes his status as a historian of a nation.

This status is confirmed by another anecdote concerning Damianus a Goes. He also wrote on Ethiopians, and Arias Montano celebrated this feat in an epigram:

> Gentis Thucydides enarrat gesta Pelasgae
> Romana claret Livius historia
> Hic alia ut taceam sera data scripta senecta
> Aethiopum accepit nomen ab historia

> Thucydides tells the history of the Greeks; Livy is famous for his Roman history: a Goes received his name from his history of the Ethiopians, to pass over the other writings of his old age.

In other words the contribution of Greek writers of Greek history to the development of humanistic national history seems to me an open question.

It is open because Renaissance scholars no longer realised what was obvious to ancient readers, namely, that neither Thucydides nor Xenophon nor other writers of *Hellenica* were historians of Greece. They were, and were considered to be, writers of contemporary or near-contemporary history which embraced events of more than one Greek state without ever involving the whole of the Greek nation. Thucydides and Xenophon were in fact historians of a brief period of history and were chiefly interested in describing and explaining changes in the balance of power between leading Greek states. There existed, of course, in Greek literature continuous narrations of the political events of individual Greek states from the origins. Especially in the fourth and third centuries B.C. scholars produced local histories of Athens, Sparta, Boeotia, Thessaly, and Sicily from the beginnings. But they never had the prestige of real historians, they never competed with Thucydides,

Xenophon, and Theopompus. They were treated as collectors of local curiosities and, in fact, tended to be antiquarians. Perhaps one of these local historians, Philistus, the fourth-century historian of Sicily, reached the level immediately below that of the "great" historians, but the best compliment he received was to be called "the little Thucydides." Local history remained an inferior intellectual activity.

There was, however, one "great" historian who tried to write the history of the Greek nation from its beginnings. This was Ephorus, the schoolfellow of Theopompus at the School of Isocrates. But the Greek nation was never a political entity, not even in the fourth century at the time of Philip of Macedon when Ephorus wrote. Consequently Ephorus shaped his history in such a way as to include large sections of non-Greek events and was considered a universal historian, not a historian of Greece, by Polybius, a good judge (V, 33, 2).

Greek historians practised pure national history only in so far as they wrote about barbarian nations or encouraged barbarians to write about themselves—either in Greek or in their own native languages. If we wanted to follow in detail the formation of the study of national history in the Graeco-Roman world, we would have to examine the whole of the extant fragments of what was the very large ethnographic literature of the Greeks. But it is evident that the Greeks produced their most spectacular results on the subject of national history when they persuaded the Romans on the one side and the Jews and Christians on the other side to write their histories according to models at least partially Greek. The Christians were a peculiar nation, yet undoubtedly a nation. It is no accident, therefore, that the Late Antique national histories took their cue from Roman and from Jewish-Christian historiography. The former was supported by the political prestige of Rome, the latter corresponded to the religious situation of the time. Both, one must add, were the result of the encounter of Greek historical thought with strong national traditions.

The strength of the biblical tradition is in no need of illustration here. I shall, therefore, devote the second part of these observations to the clarification of the situation in which the Romans created their own national history and consequently contributed to the formation of mediaeval and modern national history. The circumstances are more

curious and complex than is usually recognised. The central figure is
Fabius Pictor, the first historian of Rome.

V

If you and I read and occasionally write history, we owe this habit
to a Roman who decided to write history in the Greek manner between circa 215 and 200 B.C. His attempt to produce a Roman history
on Greek lines was part of the upheaval which we call the Second Punic
War.

Quintus Fabius Pictor belonged to a distinguished branch of a great
family, the gens Fabia, which owed the surname Pictor to an ancestor
who had painted the Temple of the Goddess Salus about 300 B.C. Roman tribal customs did not encourage patricians to become painters,
even if they confined their painting to religious subjects. In his youth
our Fabius did the things a Roman aristocrat was supposed to do. He
fought against the Gauls about 225 B.C. (Eutropius III, 5; Orosius IV,
13, 6; Plin. *N. H.* X, 71) and probably went on fighting against Hannibal, if he was not too old for that. His embassy to Delphi after Can-
nae in 216 marks the new direction of his activity. He was sent there
to consult a Greek oracle at an anxious time for Rome (Liv. XXII, 57,
5; XXIII, 11, 1–6). He was probably also asked to sound out Greek
public opinion in relation to the alliance between Philip V of Macedon
and Hannibal. Clearly he must already have been known for his broad-
minded piety, interest in Greek civilisation, knowledge of Greek, and
his diplomatic qualities. We know that he was a senator, but we have
no direct evidence that he was a member of priestly colleges. Modern
scholars have even attributed to him the forgery of Sibylline oracles,
but in doing so they have gone beyond what can reasonably be conjectured. The prestige of his family, which later claimed descent from
Hercules, would have been sufficient to give him access to priestly records in any case. After his solemn return from Delphi, of which Livy
furnishes a characteristic description, nothing more is heard of him.
He was the first Roman to piece together a connected account of the
history of his own city when he published his work in the Greek lan-

guage towards the end of the third century B.C., either during or after the Second Punic War.

We speak of the Hellenisation of Roman culture in the third century B.C. Of course there was such a process. But it was not without some very strange episodes. Twice, in 228 and in 216 B.C., the Romans consulted the Sibylline Books and were told to bury alive a couple of Greeks and a couple of Gauls. No satisfactory explanation has yet been offered for this double sacrifice. In 228 the Romans may have felt the Celtic danger, but had no quarrel with the Greeks. In 216 Hannibal was at the gates, but neither Greeks nor Gauls were a menace. The Romans never killed Carthaginians for religious purposes. It is, however, impossible to dismiss the thought that the sacrifice of two Greeks and two Gauls must have had some connection with past events of Roman history. The Celts had haunted the Romans for a long time, and the Greeks were the enemies of the Trojans and consequently of the Romans. With these sacrifices the Romans must have tried to placate hostile forces of the past. At the same time, they were also trying to invoke favourable forces of the past. In 217 the dictator Fabius Maximus promised to consecrate a temple to Venus Erycina. Eryx was the Sicilian sanctuary connected with the legend of Aeneas, and Venus was Aeneas' mother. An allusion to the Trojan past of Rome was clearly implied. In 207 attention turned to Juno Regina, the goddess whom the Romans had successfully transferred from Veii to Rome in their mortal struggle against the neighbouring city. Finally, we note that the introduction of the cult of Magna Mater from Asia in 204 was connected by ancient sources—such as Virgil (*Aen.* I, 68; IX, 80) and Ovid (*Fasti* IV, 251)—with the Trojan origins of Rome. We have no direct evidence that the Romans were aware of this connection in 204 B.C., but the connection would certainly account for the introduction of the cult into Rome.

We may well think the Romans slightly inconsistent if, in the same year 216 in which they killed a pair of Greeks, they sent Fabius to Delphi to enlist the help of a Greek oracle. True, Apollo had been a pro-Trojan god, but that was long ago. Delphi was the religious centre of Greece. In the following years Apollo was honoured in Rome by games of a Greek type (*ludi Apollinares*). Later, in 207, the ceremonies in honour of Juno—an anti-Trojan goddess—culminated in the hymn sung in the Greek fashion by twenty-seven girls. The composer of the hymn was Livius Andronicus, the Grand Old Man behind the Hellenisation of Roman poetry.

There may also be a Greek element in the introduction of the cult of Mens in 217 B.C. Wissowa interpreted it as a tribute to the Greek idea of Sophrosyne. The explanation is not certain. "Mens"—steadiness of mind—played a part in archaic Roman thought. But I do not see how one could separate the introduction of the cult of Mens in 217 from the appeal to the Apolline wisdom of Delphi in 216.

On the level of confused emotions, cruel and superstitious ceremonies, vague longings for something new and wise, the Romans were probing their Trojan past and their Greek connections. Fabius himself was not above the punctilious performance of religious rites. To hear Livy, who may go back to an autobiographical note in Fabius' annals, Fabius wore a laurel wreath throughout his journey back from Delphi to Rome: such had been the recommendation of the temple authorities. Yet Fabius did not remain on the level of his contemporaries. Instead of simply reacting to the past in terms of religious ceremonies, he tried to explore it. Instead of simply consulting the god of Delphi, he constructed a picture of Roman religion in its evolution. The superstitious awe of the past he transformed into an urge for knowledge. By directing contemporary emotions into the channel of historical research, he became the first historian of Rome. He turned what would have been one of the innumerable episodes of human gullibility into an intellectual achievement.

Fabius was not alone in this effort to piece together the various stages of Roman history. But there is some difficulty in defining the contribution of the other partners. Ancient sources are unanimous in regarding Fabius as the first of the Roman historians, and there is no reason to depart from this opinion. As for the senator Cincius Alimentus, a praetor in 211 and a prisoner of war of Hannibal, we must assume that he was younger than Fabius and that he imitated him in his history of Rome written in Greek. The real puzzle is Cn. Naevius. He was older than Fabius, fought in the First Punic War, and late in life wrote a historical poem about it. There are undeniable similarities between him and Fabius. Both wrote mainly on the origins of Rome and on contemporary events and gave little space to the intermediate period. On the other hand in the extant fragments there is no sign of Naevius' dependence on Fabius or vice versa. We are told that Naevius made Romulus a grandson of Aeneas, whereas Fabius took Romulus to be the grandson of Numitor. All that we can say at present is that both Fabius and Naevius shared in the effort to give an account of Rome's past. Naevius, however, by choosing to write a poem rather than a history, did not submit the Roman past to the process of rational elucidation in the interest of truth which is characteristic of Greek historiography. Both Naevius and Fabius tried to give the Romans an image of their own past, but Fabius was the only one to construct the image according to the principles of Greek historiographical methods.

VI

It is significant that Fabius wrote in Greek, while the contemporary poet Naevius wrote in Latin. Livius Andronicus had shown that it was possible to turn Latin into a language for poetry of the Greek type, and Naevius followed him. It would have been easy for Fabius to accept their example and to create a Latin historical style. In fields other than history Latin literary prose had been in existence for at least a century. A speech by Appius Claudius had been written down in 280 B.C. and remained in circulation long afterwards. The funeral speech by Q. Caecilius Metellus for his father in 220 was another famous piece. Juridical texts were of course common, not to speak of the Chronicle of the Pontiffs to which we shall soon return. A Latin style for history of the Greek type was within easy reach. Fabius preferred to write in a foreign language.

I am stating as a fact that Fabius wrote in Greek because Cicero (*De div.* I, 43) and Dionysius of Halicarnassus (I, 6, 2) say so categorically. But before I continue, I must add that in other passages Cicero (*De leg.* I, 6) refers to Latin annals by Fabius, and there are a few quotations from Fabius (e.g., Aulus Gellius V, 4, 3) that can only come from a Latin text. None of our sources suggests that Fabius wrote both in

Greek and in Latin, but neither does any of them suggest explicitly that the Fabius of the Latin history was a different man. I do not know of any satisfactory explanation of the evidence such as we have it. Friedrich Leo toyed with the idea that Fabius, after having published his history in Greek, left behind a draft in Latin which was edited after his death. Others have more plausibly assumed that the Greek work was later translated into Latin: we have other instances of such translations. What can hardly be doubted is that Fabius intended to publish his history in Greek and did so. We cannot say why he did so—we have no evidence—but we can at least clarify the implications of his choice. Our discussion will turn on three points: (1) what types of chronicles Rome possessed before Fabius; (2) in what company Fabius came to find himself through writing in Greek; (3) how Fabius envisaged his work as a historian of Rome.

VII

Tradition knows of two types of historical compositions existing in Rome before Fabius, and we shall have to consider them in turn. One was represented by the banquet songs, the other by the Chronicle of the Pontiffs.

Cato mentioned the banquet songs in honour of great men as an obsolete custom—something which used to happen many generations before him (Cic., *Brut.* 19, 75). Varro, too, knew of the banquet songs, and to all appearances Cato was not his source (Nonnius Marcellus p. 107 L.). Varro has different details which we must regard as independent confirmation. Cicero read about the songs in Cato's *Origines* and regretted their disappearance (*Tusc. Disp.* IV, 2, 3).

As is well known, Jacobus Perizonius was the first to see in the banquet songs a potential source for the Roman annalists. Without knowing of his seventeenth-century predecessor, Niebuhr later made the banquet songs the cornerstone of his interpretation of early Roman history. According to him the Romans' legends of their origins were the product of popular poets: the annalists, beginning with Fabius Pictor, would have derived their tales from them. Macaulay's *Lays* were the consequence. Niebuhr's theory was soon rejected and discredited by

Mommsen, and there have been scholars who have doubted the very existence of the banquet songs. But De Sanctis revived Niebuhr's theory at the beginning of this century. It became a characteristic feature of modern Italian studies on Roman literature and history, as the works by Ciaceri, Pareti, and Rostagni show. Thanks to Bowra's *Heroic Poetry* the ballad theory is now back in Macaulay's country.

I see no serious reason for doubting that the Romans had their banquet songs. But I do not believe that they exercised a strong influence on the historical tradition.

The main objection generally raised against the existence of the banquet songs in Rome is that Cato spoke of them as no longer existing. How could he have known that they had existed? Questions of this kind are always dangerous. How can we know how Cato would know? A very plausible suggestion can, however, be made as to Cato's possible channels of information.

Decemviral legislation included a law against "mala carmina," obnoxious songs. The nature of these carmina is a matter of dispute among modern scholars and was already a source of doubt for the ancients. But if you have to decide which carmina are obnoxious, you must know which carmina are permissible. I suggest that the Roman jurists discussed the various types of carmina and thereby transmitted the knowledge of the existence of banquet carmina. The first eminent commentator on the Twelve Tables, Sextus Aelius Catus, wrote about 200 B.C. He may well have been Cato's source of information. Mediaeval analogies take us even a step further. Banquet songs to celebrate heroes might easily be turned into songs to castigate enemies. Icelandic legislation prohibited almost every kind of poem on individuals in order to prevent the composition of satirical poems. I should not be surprised if there had been in Rome some direct connection between the decline of banquet songs and the rise of decemviral legislation on "mala carmina."

So much for the existence of the banquet songs and one possible cause of their decline. But Fabius Pictor preceded Cato by only one generation. What was lost many generations before Cato must also be considered lost for Fabius. There is clearly a strong reason a priori for doubting that the carmina were available to Fabius, even if we are prepared to believe that a member of the gens Fabia would accept as authoritative carmina celebrating members of other families. This argument a priori can be reinforced by a piece of direct evidence.

The presupposition of the banquet song theory is that unknown poets canonised the Roman legends before the annalists stepped in: hence the annalists received the canonical tales from the poets. Now in one case involving Fabius we can prove that the canonical tale is later than the rise of Roman historiography. In the last century of the Republic a well-defined tradition circulated about Coriolanus. Dionysius, who tells the story at great length, volunteers the information that Romulus, Remus, and Coriolanus were celebrated in hymns (I, 79, 10; 8, 62). He does not say whether the hymns were ancient nor whether they were banquet songs. We cannot use his text as proof of the rediscovery of ancient banquet songs in the age of Augustus. But we must assume that there was no disagreement between the contents of these hymns and the current legend of Coriolanus: the disagreement would have been noticed. Indeed Livy noticed that Fabius had a version of his own of Coriolanus' story (II, 40, 10). While in the traditional story the Volsci killed Coriolanus when he refused to lead them against Rome, in Fabius' version Coriolanus died an old man in exile. According to Fabius, Coriolanus once remarked that exile was more painful in old age. It is therefore clear that the ordinary version was not yet canonical before Fabius. If there were hymns about Coriolanus, either they were later than Fabius or they did not affect him. The legends of early Rome were still evolving in the age of Fabius and became stereotyped only in the second, or perhaps in the first, century B.C. The theory of the banquet songs explains very few of the facts known to us about early Roman tradition. There is certainly no reason to believe that Fabius used them.

The Annals of the Pontiffs were a much more solid reality in the time of Fabius. To begin with, they existed. Second, whatever they may have contained, they were annals. They ordered their material according to years and gave the names of the consuls of each year. In adopting the annalistic form and the consular dates Fabius evidently had the example of the pontiffs before him. Though he did his best to help his Greek readers by translating some basic dates—for instance, the foundation of Rome—into Olympiads, his general system of chronology is Roman, not Greek. The real question is whether the pontifical Annals could give him more than the names of the consuls.

As is well known, the pontiffs registered what mattered to them on a whitewashed board, the *tabula dealbata*, which was changed every year and had the form of a calendar. Everyone was free to inspect it. At the end of each year the contents of the relevant *tabula* must have been transcribed into a scroll or a codex and automatically became part of a chronicle which presumably preserved the calendar form. Finally, this chronicle was put into order and apparently published in eighty volumes at the end of the second century B.C.

Cato the Censor thought that a historian would not find much useful information in the Annals of the Pontiffs (Aulus Gellius II, 28, 6). According to him they recorded only famines, eclipses, and other portents. Cato was a difficult character and liked to be outrageous. But he is very precise in his indictment, and his evidence cannot be dismissed lightly. He says that the Annals did not give any direct information about military and political events. Cato is contradicted by Cicero and Servius, who state more or less definitely that the pontiffs registered military and political events. Cicero says that the "pontifex maximus res omnis singulorum annorum mandabat litteris" (*De or.* II, 52), and his context shows that he means military and political events. Servius is even more specific: the registration included "domi militiaeque terra marique gesta per singulos dies" (Serv. Dan. ad Verg. *Aen.* I, 373).

The contradiction between Cato and Cicero does not necessarily imply that one of them must be wrong. Both may be right, if they refer to different stages in the evoluton of the Annals. Cato wrote before the final edition and publication of the Annals about 120 B.C.; Cicero and the source of Servius (perhaps Verrius Flaccus) wrote after their publication. We may well ask whether this circumstance is not likely to account for the contradiction between them and Cato. It is obvious that publication would in any case necessitate a certain amount of editorial work. Notes hurriedly put down in different centuries could not be published without revision. The very evolution of the Latin language made the revision imperative. If we now consider the discrepancy between Cato and Cicero-Servius about the nature of pontifical registration, we may suspect that editorial intervention was drastic and far-reaching. Did the editors take to heart Cato's complaint and act accordingly? The military and political events were exactly what Cato missed and Cicero and the source of Servius found in the records of the pontiffs.

So far, of course, we have stated a mere hypothesis. But there are hard facts which prove that at some stage (not necessarily at the moment of publication about 120 B.C.) the Annals of the Pontiffs were manipulated, enlarged, and falsified. We know from Cicero that the Annals of the Pontiffs began with the origins of the city—*ab initio rerum Romanarum*. Unless we are prepared to attribute to Romulus an unusual gift of foresight, it is clear that the earlier part of the Annals was a later addition. Then we read in the so-called *Origo gentis Romanae* that the first four books of the Annals of the Pontiffs were concerned with events earlier than Romulus (17, 3; 5). The *Origo* has a bad reputation as regards reliability, but this piece of information deserves credence. Basically it agrees with Cicero's formula *ab initio rerum Romanarum*, which may include the Alban stage of Roman history (or prehistory). It also tallies with the enormous number, eighty, of the books of the whole work. Granted the reliability of the *Origo gentis Romanae* on this point, we must assume that at a certain moment an editor extended the Annals to embrace the legendary phase of Alba Longa. Finally, we have some direct evidence that the authentic part of the Annals cannot have started much before the year 350 *ab urbe condita*. We know from Cicero (*De rep*. I, 16, 25) that in that year the *Annales maximi* made the first registration of an eclipse. I shall not discuss the chronological questions involved. It will be enough to say that his date is plausible in so far as it takes us to about 400 B.C., not long before the destruction of Rome by the Gauls. The pontiffs probably lost their archives on that occasion, but they may easily have reconstructed the lost *tabulae*, combining the events of the last few years preceding the disaster. There was a total eclipse in 400 B.C. which was certainly not forgotten by 390.

To sum up this discussion: it is evident that the Annals of the Pontiffs were manipulated. Their reliable section can hardly have included much material referring to events earlier than 400 B.C. We do not

know when the interpolations were made. But the disagreement between Cato and Cicero about the contents of the Annals makes me suspect that the most serious interpolations were made about 120 B.C. If
this hypothesis is correct, we must assume that the editors of the *Annales maximi* availed themselves of the various books of history produced in the late third century and during the second century (Fabius
Pictor, Cincius Alimentus, Cato, Cassius Hemina, etc.) in order to en-
large the scope of their work and to fill the lacunae of the older *tabulae*. There is nothing impossible in the amusing suggestion that the
pontiffs, after having contributed to the rise of Roman historiography,
ransacked the works of the Roman historians to improve their own
Annals before publication.

On this hypothesis the Annals, or rather the registrations, accessible
to Fabius were much poorer in content than those known to Cicero.
They provided the essential chronological framework. They must have
mentioned defeats, victories, wars, and peace treaties whenever such
events occasioned religious ceremonies or were connected with portents. But they did not yet regularly record military and political
events. Fabius would not have been able to piece together from such
facts as they contained a coherent account of the history of Rome before the First Punic War. Nor would he have found recorded in them
those individual heroic actions which are an essential part of early Roman tradition. Whatever view we take of the pontifical registrations
available to Fabius, we must at least agree that Mucius Scaevola, Coriolanus, Manlius Capitolinus, and other heroes were unlikely to have
been included.

VIII

It would seem evident that Fabius decided to write in Greek because
the Roman historical tradition struck him as unsatisfactory. The banquet songs were probably no longer in existence: he could have only a
vague idea of their contents. The registrations of the pontiffs certainly
existed and were valuable to him. But they seemed restricted in scope,
disconnected in character, repellent in style, as soon as they were compared with the works of the Greek historians. To read Greek historical

books was to discover not only that the Greeks practised a different type of historiography, but that they had already taught other nations to write history in Greek in the Greek way and, furthermore, that they had something specific to say about Rome itself.

In the third century, when Greek was the official language of civilisation from Judaea to Spain, everyone tried to write history in Greek. The Greeks more than ever wrote about other nations, and the other nations in their turn were stimulated to write about themselves in Greek according to Greek standards. As I have already mentioned, under the impact of Hellenisation the natives of many countries were persuaded to *re*think their national history and to present it in the Greek language to the educated readers of a multinational society. Fabius was in a large, and not always very select, company when writing his Greek annals.

Manetho wrote Egyptian history and Berossus wrote Babylonian history, both in Greek, in the first part of the third century B.C. Internationalism did not exclude nationalism. Manetho wanted to show up the incompetence of Herodotus. The development continued in the second half of the century and involved new nations. The Jews produced a Greek translation of the Bible. Then a certain Demetrius who lived under Ptolemy IV, towards the end of the century, summarised biblical history and tried to be precise in chronology. Flavius Josephus believed that Demetrius was a pagan and may even have confused him with Demetrius Phalereus (*c. Apion.* I, 218). Internal evidence and the testimony of Eusebius (*Praep. Ev.* IX, 21) leave no doubt that he was a Jew. There is good reason to believe that Menander of Ephesus was Demetrius' contemporary. Like him Menander was trained in the methods of Alexandrian scholarship. Menander wrote Phoenician history (Jos., *c. Apion.* I, 116). Nobody tells us that he was a Phoenician by origin, but he used native chronicles and apparently claimed to have translated them into Greek. Perhaps Menander was no more of a Greek than Zeno the Stoic was.

Demetrius was certainly, and Menander probably, a contemporary of Fabius Pictor. In comparison with them Fabius was exceptional only in the sense that he wrote the history of a state the rulers of which were not Greek. But if we knew more, we would probably recognise that even in this limited sense he was not really an exception. Etruscan histories existed and were used by Greek and Roman historians. It is at least conceivable that some of them were written in Greek.

We should not be far from the truth if we said that Fabius wrote history in Greek because everybody else was doing so. But there is something more to add. Greek was not only the language of historiography: it had already become, before Fabius, the language in which specific information about Rome could be obtained. We can overlook for the present purpose the information about certain events of Roman history with international repercussions, such as the occupation of Rome by the Gauls, that had found its way into works by Theopompus, Heraclides Ponticus, Aristotle, and Theophrastus. But in the third century B.C. one Greek historian set out to become the source of information for anyone interested in the West and more particularly in Rome.

With patient work which lasted for fifty years Timaeus of Tauromenium tried to satisfy the curiosity of his contemporaries about the West. We may even suggest that he did much to shape and direct their curiosity. A political exile from Sicily, he lived for the greater part of his life in Athens, from about 315 to about 265 B.C., and devoted himself single-mindedly to the task of writing a history of the West. He centred his work on Sicily, but extended his research to the whole of Italy, Gaul, Spain, Libya, and even touched on the Northern countries, about which he trusted Pytheas. Whereas he gave a complete political history of Sicily, he confined himself to the geography and ethnography of the other countries. Obviously he was following the example of Herodotus, with appropriate adaptations.

Timaeus was a pedant, was inclined to criticise his predecessors violently, had political prejudices, and made books out of books. In a word, he was one of us. Like many of us he also travelled, questioned natives, and quoted original documents. He talked about Rome, perhaps in the lost first books of his work, within the framework of his ethnographical research.

He had not yet finished his history of Sicily when an event of importance confirmed that he had been right in turning his attention to the West. The Romans became involved in a war with Pyrrhus. About 275 B.C. they proved their superiority over a Hellenistic army and made it clear that the Hellenistic monarchies had no chance of expanding in the Western direction. The victory of the Romans was bound to create a sensation in the Greek world. A contemporary of Timaeus, Lycophron, expressed his surprise in the poem *Alexandra*, which modern critics have vainly tried to relegate to the second century B.C. Hieronymus of Cardia considered it necessary to give a brief summary of Roman history within the context of his history of the Hellenistic kings, which included Pyrrhus. But Timaeus himself, though old, was alert enough to produce an appendix to his history, containing an account of the wars of Pyrrhus in Italy. He was not satisfied with a mere factual history. He went back to earlier stages of Roman political and cultural history. He followed up the developments of Roman policy until the outbreak of the First Punic War. The evidence, such as we have it, does not encourage the belief that Timaeus gave more than a rapid survey of the rise of Rome to the status of a great power. Timaeus is never referred to by our authorities for details of Roman political history. But the mere fact that he was the first to devote a book to a war between Greeks and Romans represented a revolution: the more so because he was so interested in the customs and legends of Rome. His information was good. He was able to get some of his facts from natives of Lavinium (fr. 59 Jacoby). Excavations have proved that in the fourth century B.C., Lavinium had a mixed Hellenic-Latin culture and was therefore a place for contacts between Greeks and Latins. Timaeus' work naturally became a landmark. Lycophron and Callimachus used him as one of their sources for the West. Fifty years after Fabius, Timaeus' work continued to be so much admired that Polybius was alarmed. He felt that in order to establish himself before his Roman public he had to make a determined effort to discredit his predecessor. Though he devoted a whole book to this enterprise, Varro and Cicero still read their Timaeus with attention and apparent relish.

Even the meagre fragments of Fabius' annals show that he learned from Timaeus. Interest in national customs, religious ceremonies, picturesque and anecdotal details, is as evident in Fabius as it is in Timaeus. His Greek dates are in Olympic years, as we would expect from an admirer of Timaeus. The cultural side of Fabius' annals is unthinkable without the example of Timaeus. The long description of the *ludi magni*, the fragment on the history of the alphabet, the notes on the integrity of the Roman magistrates and on the severity of Roman "mores," recall Timaeus. He gave Fabius the taste for the happy turn of phrase, for the significant anecdote, for the antiquarian detail, and perhaps even for the autobiographical elements.

But Timaeus was not the only Greek whom Fabius studied. As Professor E. J. Bickerman has taught us in a memorable article (*Class. Philol.* 47, 1952, 65–81), the Greeks were specialists in the problems of national origins. They formulated the problems, collected the evidence, and reached conclusions for each nation. They created a special literary genre, the "foundation of cities." Something about Aeneas' arrival in Italy and the founding of Rome had already been said by Hellanicus at the end of the fifth century B.C. The origins of Rome continued to intrigue the Greeks in the fourth century before they became seriously interested in the development of the Roman state. We now know from a catalogue of historical books contained in an inscription from Taormina that Fabius spoke of the arrival of Hercules in Italy and mentioned the founder of Lanuvium as a companion of Aeneas (G. Manganaro, *La Parola del Passato* 29, 1974, 394–396): this reminds us immediately of Greek forms of narration. It is also our good fortune to know that Fabius admitted that a substantially correct version of the native legend of Romulus and Remus could be read in a Greek historian, Diocles of Peparethus. Plutarch in a famous passage of his Life of Romulus (III, 1) emphatically asserts that Fabius followed the account given by Diocles. Modern scholars have tried to undermine his statement mainly on the grounds that no Roman would go to a Greek historian for a trustworthy account of the origins of his own city. But this argument can easily be reversed, and there are other arguments in favour of Diocles' priority. First, we know from another source that Diocles lived well before 150 B.C. and cast his net rather wide, having also written on Persia. Second, the discovery of an inscription from Chios has confirmed that the Greeks were familiar with the legend of Romulus and Remus not long after 200 B.C. So far the inscription, though known for at least twenty years, has been only partially published (N. M. Kontoleon, *Akte IV. Int. Kongr. Epigraphik* 1962, 1964, 192).

It is in honour of a man who, among other things, set up some sort of monument with a representation "of the birth of the founder of Rome Romulus and of his brother Remus." If the legend of Romulus and Remus was current in a rather remote part of the Greek world not long after 200 B.C., there is nothing remarkable in the fact that Diocles should have been writing about it twenty or thirty years earlier, in time to be used by Fabius. Fabius paid homage to the mastery of the Greeks in the matter of origins by accepting what they had written. Later Romans agreed with him. They kept their national legend in the Greek dress transmitted by Fabius and found it so congenial that they seldom thought of improving on it. Real disagreements with the story told by Fabius remained individual aberrations. To mention one, there was a certain writer, Egnatius, who ventured to suggest that Remus survived Romulus. His opinion is recorded only in the disreputable *Origo gentis Romanae*.

IX

There is no suggestion that Fabius simply capitulated before the Greek historians. He tried to strike a balance between the native traditions and the Greek accounts. That he could be independent in his judgement is shown by his choice of a date for the foundation of Rome which is at variance with Timaeus. Being a Fabius, he was not likely to disregard the oral traditions and the written documents of his own family and of allied aristocratic families. The atrium of his own house with its *imagines maiorum* and relative *elogia* must have been his principal archive. Several of the few extant fragments show that he used the traditions of his own family. This would be only natural both for the wars of the early Republic (before the battle of the Cremera when his family faced ruin) and for the Samnite wars. In their family traditions the Fabii were in no danger of being parochial. Just as in the third century they were the first to acquire Greek language and culture, so in the fourth century they had sent their children to Caere to learn Etruscan language and literature. The great Fabius Rullianus had been aided in his invasion of Etruria by a brother, "Caere educatus apud hospites, Etruscis inde litteris eruditus," who knew Etruscan well (Liv. IX, 36, 9). The Etruscan *hospites* may well have told the Fabii something about the days in which Etruscan kings had ruled Rome—not necessarily the truth.

Yet the clearest proof of the influence of Greek models is that Fabius devoted the greater part of his history to the origins of Rome and to contemporary events. The origins and the wars with Pyrrhus and with Carthage were the sections of Roman history that had interested the Greeks. Fabius must have thought that he could not afford to be diffuse on subjects which the Greeks had left unexplored. Indeed he was too clever to idealise even his own ancestors. His version of the famous quarrel between the dictator L. Papirius and the *magister equitum* Fabius Rullianus in the year 325 B.C. was not entirely favourable to the latter. He stated, either whimsically or brutally, that Fabius Rullianus burned the booty in order to prevent the dictator from using it to adorn his own triumph (Liv. VIII, 30, 3).

To sum up, Fabius made his own the methods and results of Greek historians and extended them to periods and aspects of Roman history which the Greeks had not studied much. In doing so, he used a Roman chronological system and no doubt took advantage of the pontifical Annals and other Roman sources. He was not, however, able to collect many new facts for the periods of Roman history which had not been treated previously by the Greeks.

It will have been noticed that, so far, I have not even alluded to the now fashionable theory that Fabius wrote in Greek in order to make propaganda on behalf of Rome among Greeks. There was certainly plenty of scope for the presentation of the Roman case to the Greeks during or after the Second Punic War. Philinus of Agrigentum had probably already published his history of the First Punic War which was favourable to the Carthaginians. Hannibal had taken care to have two Greek historians in his camp: Silenus of Calacte and Sosylus of Sparta. Another Greek historian, Chaereas, is mentioned by Polybius (III, 20, 5) in a context which seems to imply that he was favourable to Hannibal. Even if Silenus and Sosylus published their work after Fabius, he must have known while he was writing that Hannibal had

Greek historians in his service. There is no difficulty in believing that Fabius was conscious of helping Rome when he undertook to write in Greek.

But before you use history to make propaganda you must know how to write history. The important fact about Fabius is not that he wrote history for propaganda but that he wrote history at all. Furthermore, where is the evidence for Fabius' propaganda?

All we can say for certain is that Polybius considered Fabius and Philinus the most authoritative historians of the First Punic War respectively from the Roman and from the Carthaginian point of view: he criticised both for being biased. There is a difference between bias and propaganda.

In the few cases in which Fabius is quoted about contemporary events, he looks, perhaps deceptively, objective and serene. He gave a precise list of the allied forces that helped Rome to beat the Gauls in 225 B.C.: such a catalogue was in the best tradition of Greek historiography. He developed the view that in the First Punic War both Rome and Carthage were almost exhausted before the last battle. He also assumed that there was a conflict between Hannibal and the other Carthaginian leaders and that the former forced the hands of the latter at the time of the Saguntum affair. This was an interpretation which Polybius was unable to share. It may well be wrong, but it shows that Fabius was in no hurry to present the Carthaginians to the Greek public as collectively responsible for the beginning of the Second Punic War. The man who decided to check the national Chronicle of the Pontiffs against the histories of the Greeks obviously had the freedom of mind that is incompatible with mere propaganda. If we have no reason to think that Fabius was a vulgar propagandist, we have even less reason to think that he invented stories about the Roman past. Professor A. Alföldi worked hard to present Fabius as a shameless forger. He is far from convincing. His suggestion that Cloelia, Lucretia, and other heroic women of Roman history must have been invented by Fabius because women had no place in genuine Roman tradition seems to me without any foundation whatsoever and incidentally is partly due to a wrong inference from what I once wrote about the banquet songs.

The best test of a historian's honesty is what he says about his own family. Now Fabius had good grounds for believing that his ancestors were Romulus' contemporaries. The Luperci Fabiani—obviously a religious corporation connected with the Fabian family—were considered as ancient as the Roman *urbs*. Yet the striking thing about our tradition on the Fabii is that it is silent about their activities, if any, in the monarchic period. This means, of course, that no authentic recollection had been preserved of the prerepublican Fabii, but it also means that Fabius Pictor did not try to remedy the deficiencies of the tradition by inventions of his own. Fabius certainly formed a lofty picture of Rome in the age of the kings (Liv. I, 44, 2; Dion. Hal. IV, 15, 1). He reported an alleged census of Servius which counted eighty thousand male citizens liable for militay service ("qui arma ferre possent"). He also attributed thirty local tribes to the Servian city. This is a picture with which we may well find it impossible to agree. But apart from the fact that the Fabii do not figure in it, there are other reasons why we should not consider it a piece of Pictor's private fantasy. The reforms of Servius had already been described by Timaeus, who committed the enormous anachronism of ascribing the introduction of coinage to this king. Timaeus had no mean opinion of the importance of Rome under Servius. Elsewhere I have tried to show that in his interpretation of the numbers of the Servian census Fabius Pictor may have accepted a figure already given by Timaeus, though disagreeing with its explanation (*Terzo Contributo* II, 654). If Fabius indulged in a complacent picture of early Rome, he was not alone in this.

In the anonymous Greek fragment which is known as the *Ineditum Vaticanum*, there is a strange speech by a Roman called Keson, who warns the Carthaginians not to rely on their supremacy at sea (A. B. Drachmann, *Diodors Römische Annalen . . . samt dem Ineditum Vaticanum*, Bonn, 1912). In the past the Romans had been able to adopt the military techniques of the Etruscans and of the Samnites: in the same way they would deal with the Carthaginians. H. von Arnim recognised in the name Keson the prenomen Kaeso typical of the Fabian family and conjectured that Fabius Pictor was the ultimate source of the story (*Hermes* 27, 1892, 130). Though others have suggested the name of Posidonius as the source of the *Ineditum Vaticanum*, I still think that von Arnim's conjecture is more probable. The speech by Keson looks like an authentic piece of Fabius' philosophy of history. If it was propaganda, it was not propaganda based on lies and forgery. In the Greek manner it was put in the form of a speech.

X

Other Romans followed Fabius in his attempt to write Roman history in the Greek language. But soon Cato showed that it was possible to use the Latin language for a historiography of the Greek type. His *Origines* were Latin in language and Greek in spirit. I assume that under the influence of Cato somebody decided to translate Fabius' annals into Latin. What happened at any rate is that during the second century B.C. historiography of the Greek type but written in Latin became current in Rome.

Fabius really started a new era when he summoned the Greek historians to help him to put order into the Roman tradition. This had positive and negative consequences. The positive consequence of his operation was that forever after the Romans had the resources of Greek historiography at their disposal. Even the pontifical registrations were soon to cease, being out of touch with the new spirit. The political judgement, the source criticism, the stylistic devices of the Roman historians, were permanently affected by the Greek models. Sallust looked back to Thucydides, Livy exploited Polybius, Varro took advantage of the Greek antiquarians. The Romans were compelled by Greek example to probe their history from various angles—the political, the biographical, the erudite.

The main negative consequences of the Roman assimilation of Greek historiography were two. The first was that the Romans inherited the Greek inability to do real research on the intermediate period between origins and contemporary events. Like the Greeks the Roman historians remained essentially equipped either to collect and criticise mythical traditions or to observe and report contemporary history. They were hardly able to examine the historical as opposed to the mythical past, if by examination we mean a systematic (not an occasional) study of primary evidence. They could collate and criticise reports by preceding historians, but their study of more remote history never had the value and the cogency of their study of contemporary events. Mediaeval and modern historians until the eighteenth and in many cases until the nineteenth century worked under the same limitation, just because they inherited the methods of Roman historiography. Machiavelli, Guicciardini, Commynes, and their followers are historians of their own times.

The second negative consequence was that Roman historiography never reacted spontaneously to the Roman past. The Romans always judged themselves with an eye to the Greeks. It is difficult to assess what this meant in the long run. After all every historian writes with an eye to his predecessors. But each Greek historian of the Classical and Hellenistic ages was more interested in what he had to say than in what his predecessors had said. If he attacked his predecessors, it was because he had to justify himself. With the Romans—or indeed with the Greeks who followed the Roman path in imperial times—one is not so sure. They were self-consciously building up their own history in the light of Greek history. To Cicero and his contemporaries only the Greeks were really capable of writing history. Quintilian implies no blame when he observes that much in Sallust was translated from the Greek (*Inst. Or.* IX, 3, 17). In starting the story of the Second Punic War, Livy leaves us in no doubt that he remembered Thucydides and the Peloponnesian War.

The Roman historians were obsessed by the comparison with the Greeks. Later, under Roman influence, the humanistic historians were obsessed by the comparison with their classical models. The historiography of Western Europe was born with Fabius Pictor as an act of liberalisation and rationalisation, but under somewhat artificial circumstances which remained characteristic of European historiography until recent times. It would be interesting to discuss at what date modern historians began to feel that comparison with the Latins and the Greeks was no longer compulsory. Perhaps in the eighteenth century, perhaps only in the nineteenth century.

We shall not blame Fabius Pictor if in his struggle against superstition and traditionalism he had to turn to the Greeks in order to discredit the Roman pontiffs. Classicism is never so dangerous as traditionalism. Moreover, the result of Fabius' efforts was perhaps more original than he expected or intended. The annals he produced inaugurated a new type of national history, less antiquarian than the local chronicles of the Greek states, more concerned with the continuity of political institutions than most of the Greek general histories we know.

The Romans could not remain bound to the notion of contemporary history because they had a profound sense of tradition and continuity. They might be uncritical about their own past, but they felt they had to narrate their own history *ab urbe condita*, from the beginnings. The annals from the origins of Rome were the most characteristic product of their historiography. Livy was the greatest representative of this genre, which was still accepted by Tacitus as the natural form of history writing. In these annals something survived of the spirit of the old pontifical registrations, the Annals of the Pontiffs. Revolutionary in a hundred ways, Fabius had remained faithful to the old spirit of Roman pre-Greek annals by starting from the immemorial past and making it memorial. Roman traditionalism had inspired the Annals of the Pontiffs. Fabius Pictor kept it alive while accepting the methods, and to a great extent the contents, of Greek political history. Fabius invented national history for the Latin West. Thereby he created the form for the expression of national consciousness: possibly he contributed to the creation of national consciousness itself, such as we understand it.

We have only to turn to Cornelius Tacitus for confirmation. Tacitus knew that he was living in a world of which the Greeks of previous ages had seen little. He was too intensely concerned with his own century to write about previous centuries, but he never forgot them: he assumed continuity in Roman history. He was original enough to establish a line of his own in the history of historiography. Freed from allegiance to Greek models, he imposed his individuality on his readers. There is a Tacitist school, in a sense in which it would be difficult to speak even of a Sallustian or Caesarian or Livian school of history.

CHAPTER FIVE

Tacitus and the Tacitist Tradition

I

For about three centuries, from the Reformation to the French Revolution, Tacitus inspired or troubled politicians, moralists, and even theologians, not to speak of the subjects he provided for poetry and painting. He operated in two different camps. First, he helped the Germans to reassert their nationality and consequently to attack the foreign rule of the Roman Church. Second, he disclosed the secrets of political behaviour both to those who governed and to those who were governed. He taught the former more than one sleight-of-hand and warned the latter that such tricks were cruel and inevitable: everyone had to know his place. Aphorisms and political discourses on Tacitean themes multiplied. There was of course also a great deal of imitation of Tacitus in historical prose. But only the German antiquarians found in Tacitus—and more specifically in the *Germania*—a precise model for their historical work. The events of modern Europe at large could not be satisfactorily narrated within a Tacitean framework. Tacitus had never dealt with geographical discoveries, colonisation, wars of religion, and trade competition. Though he had perceived the future importance of Germans and Christians, he had been spared the fulfilment of his forebodings. It is therefore more appropriate to speak of "Tacitism" in relation to the political thought of the age of absolutism, though few historians of that age remained insensitive to his art of dis-

---

The original lecture title was "Tacitus and the Discovery of Imperial Tyranny."

covering substance under appearances. On the eve of the French Revolution, Gibbon gave the supreme example of Tacitean style adapted
to a different type of historiography. Even so, Gibbon's subject was not
modern history. Whatever Tacitus' lesson for the age of absolutism, its
roots were in his own choice of subjects and in his own ambiguities.
Tacitism was not an arbitrary interpolation into Tacitus. To understand Tacitism, we must first consider Tacitus.

II

We must resist any attempt at presenting Tacitus as a researcher on
original evidence in the sense in which a historian of the twentieth century is a researcher. We know that ancient historians normally did research only in connection with contemporary events which they were
the first to describe: Pliny the Younger, a friend of Tacitus, confirms
this. Tacitus, no doubt, read with care the *acta senatus* and the *acta
diurna*—the records of the Senate meetings and the city journal—for
the period of Domitian, in which he broke new ground. But we cannot
assume without very good reasons that he did the same thing systematically for the period from Tiberius to Titus, for which he could use
literary sources. The *Histories* offer the best opportunity for examining Tacitus' methods of work. We can compare Tacitus with Suetonius,
Plutarch, and Dio on the events of the year A.D. 69. Tacitus' account is
very similar to that of the other authorities, and clearly derives from a
common source. In the *Annals* the similarities with the parallel sources
are not so close—a fact that admits of more than one explanation. But
even in the *Annals*, Tacitus claims in only one place to have gone back
to the *acta senatus* (XV, 74), whereas he implies at least twice that he
did not trouble to consult them on controversial issues. In *Annals* II,
88, Tacitus states: "I find from contemporary authors who were members of the Senate that a letter was read in the Curia from the Chattan
chief Adgandestrius promising the death of Arminius, if poison were
sent to do the work." Here Tacitus says that he got his information
from senatorial historians: he does not mention the *acta senatus*,
though the letter from the German chieftain was read in the Senate.
Mommsen tried to avoid the inevitable inference by suggesting that in

a question of political murder the *acta senatus* would remain silent. But if Tacitus had been in the habit of checking the historians against the *acta senatus*, he would have told us that the *acta senatus* did not confirm the story of the senatorial historians. In another passage, *Annals* I, 81, Tacitus admits his inability to form a clear picture of the procedure of the consular elections of A.D. 15, though he had consulted the historians and Tiberius' speeches. Here again he excludes the *acta senatus* by implication. Incidentally we must not take the reference to Tiberius' speeches as a reference to the *acta senatus*: Tiberius' speeches had been collected and could be read without going to the *acta senatus*. If a confirmation of these deductions was needed, it was provided by the discovery of the *Tabula Hebana*. The inscription contains some at least of the details about the elections which Tacitus had been unable to discover for himself. As the *Tabula Hebana* is substantially, if not formally, a deliberation of the Senate, it must have been reported in the *acta senatus*. Tacitus' ignorance of its contents can be explained only if he did not consult the relevant protocols of the Senate meetings.

Sir Ronald Syme is prepared to believe that Tacitus used the *acta senatus* to make a special study of the speeches of the Emperor Claudius. Tacitus' antiquarian excursuses would derive, not from an antiquarian handbook, as Friedrich Leo suggested, but from Claudius' antiquarian speeches in the Senate. This is an amusing thought; and there is certainly an element of truth in it. Tacitus read with great care Claudius' speech about the admission of the Gauls to the Senate because he remembered it in a different context for his excursus on Mons Caelius (*Ann.* IV, 65). We can easily believe that he took a whimsical pleasure in other pieces of Claudian pedantry. He devoted an excursus in *Annals* XI, 14 to the history of the alphabet, for instance: we know that problems connected with the alphabet were a favourite subject with the Emperor Claudius. But there is nothing to suggest that Tacitus' acquaintance with Claudius' speeches was wide. The further suggestion that Tacitus knew Claudius' speeches from direct consultation of the *acta senatus* is even less probable. One example will make my point clear. Tacitus states that Augustus preceded Claudius in enlarging the *pomerium*, that is, the sacred boundary of Rome (*Ann.* XII, 23). This statement Sir Ronald Syme takes to come from a speech by Claudius in the Senate on the proposed extension of the sacred boundary. Over-whelming evidence shows that Augustus never extended the *pomerium*. Augustus himself never mentions such a performance in his *Res Gestae*; and the *Lex de imperio Vespasiani* does not cite Augustus as a predecessor of Claudius in extending the *pomerium*. Furthermore, the respectable antiquarian who is behind Seneca in the discussion on the *pomerium* in the *De Brevitate vitae* (XIII, 8) does not know of an extension of the *pomerium* by Augustus. *De Brevitate vitae* itself was written within a few months of the extension of the *pomerium* by Claudius when the subject was topical. The only explanation for this silence is that Augustus did not in fact extend the *pomerium*. But if he did not, then Claudius is unlikely to have lied to the senators in an official speech. He was too good an antiquarian to discredit himself by inventing facts. We do not know who first made the mistake of attributing the extension of the *pomerium* to Augustus, but we can at least say that it was not Claudius. Somebody between Claudius and Tacitus must have thought fit to attribute a widening of the sacred border of Rome to the first emperor. Tacitus here depends not on the *acta senatus*, but on a literary tradition later accepted by Dio Cassius and also by the *Historia Augusta*. The extent of Tacitus' original research is bound to be a matter of doubt and controversy because only in a few cases do we have enough evidence to assess it. For instance, we cannot say where Tacitus found his information about the debate between Helvidius Priscus and Eprius Marcellus which now figures so conspicuously in the *Histories*, Book IV. He may have read about it in the *acta senatus*, but more probably in the biography of Helvidius Priscus which had been written by Herennius Senecio. Indeed Tacitus may simply have based his account on another historian who had already used the biography of Helvidius written by Herennius Senecio. What we can say is that our present evidence offers nothing to support the anachronistic image of a Tacitus passing his mornings in the archives of the Roman Senate.

If Tacitus was not a researcher in the modern sense, he was, however, a writer whose reliability cannot be seriously questioned. When we question Tacitus' account of Tiberius or doubt his information about the Parthian campaigns of Nero, we are really discussing details.

To put it more sharply, if you do not believe Livy on Romulus, this means that you cannot know anything about Romulus, but if you do not believe Tacitus on Tiberius, this means only that you have to think again about certain details of Tiberius' reign. Suetonius, Dio, Plutarch—not to speak of the inscriptions—support Tacitus in all his main facts and reduce the controversy about his truthfulness to narrow margins. While the discovery of the *Tabula Hebana* has shown that Tacitus overlooked certain aspects of the consular elections under Tiberius, we must not forget that Tacitus had admitted his inability to get sufficient information about them. I know of only one case in which Tacitus may be suspected with some justification of having consciously altered the truth for the sake of rhetorical effect. He makes Cremutius Cordus recite a speech in the Senate during his trial (*Ann.* IV, 34). Yet we know from Seneca that Cremutius Cordus committed suicide before he was tried in the Senate (*Cons. Marc.* XXII, 6). It is hard to avoid the conclusion that Tacitus made Cremutius go before the Senate because he had thought of a good speech to put into his mouth. But it is fair to add that this idea may already have occurred to a predecessor of Tacitus. In that case Tacitus would have been at fault in trusting a predecessor instead of going to read the *acta senatus* for himself.

Tacitus never claimed to be a historian with a method of his own, as Thucydides or Polybius did. The claims he makes for himself—to write *sine ira et studio* and to disdain trivial details—belong to the conventions of Graeco-Roman historiography. He accepts the pattern of Roman annalistic writing; he makes it plain that he studied his Sallust, Caesar, and Livy. He does not want to appear as an innovator. Neither the subjects he chooses nor the materials he uses were new or particularly difficult to handle.

Yet in another sense Tacitus is one of the most experimental historians of Antiquity. Only Xenophon, among the historians who have come down to us, can be compared with him in this respect. Xenophon tried biography, historical novel, military history with an autobiographical element, mere historical narrative, and finally a collection of philosophical sayings. Superficially Tacitus is not so many-sided. He tried only biography, ethnography, historical discussion of the decline of eloquence, and finally plain annalistic narrative. But almost all his experiments are complex. Each big experiment includes other experiments. The *Agricola* is biography with an ethnographic-historical background: the combination cannot have been common. The *Germania* is ethnography with a political message. I may be permitted to take the dialogue *De Oratoribus* as Tacitus' work without further discussion. It combines an attempt to describe the subjective reactions of various persons to the political regime under which they live with an attempt to clarify the causes of the decline of eloquence. Even in his most mature historical writing Tacitus experimented. What we have of the *Histories* is a picture of a civil war in which the leaders are no more and perhaps less important than the crowds—soldiers, provincials, Roman mob. In the *Annals* the perspective is changed. The personalities of the emperors and of their women, of a few generals and philosophers, dominate the scene. We take the change to be natural because Tacitus makes it appear natural, but other solutions were possible. We may suspect that the complexities of that dark emperor-maker Antonius Primus, as described in the *Histories*, would have been more interesting to Tacitus ten years later when he wrote the *Annals*; while the open-air scenes of the fire of Rome as told in the *Annals* would have been better described ten years earlier, when he wrote the *Histories*

Some of the experiments were never developed in full. The lesser works after all are lesser works just because they do no more than hint at the most serious historical problems. The *Agricola* might have developed into a study of the impact of Romanisation on the natives of Britain. The *Germania* is potentially an enquiry into the relations between the free Germans and the Roman Empire; the *Dialogus* outlines research on the interrelations between political liberty and intellectual activities. None of these themes is taken up in earnest and turned into a full-scale history. Tacitus would have become a very different type of historian if he had done so. He would have become a critic of the structure of the Roman Empire. He would have told us explicitly whether or not he believed that there was a reasonable alternative to the present regime of Rome. The very fact that Tacitus wrote the *Agricola* and the *Germania* in A.D. 98, before the *Histories* and the *Annals*, shows that at the beginning of his career as a historian he wanted to ask some fundamental questions about Roman provincial government. But he did not pursue these themes fully; nor did he develop the theme of the decline of eloquence outside the *Dialogus*. Any development of this kind would have implied a complete break with the political and historiographical tradition of Rome. Politically Tacitus would have had to give up the society of the senatorial class for which he had probably been the first member of his family to qualify. Historiographically he would have had to repudiate the traditions of Roman annalistic writing, confined as it was to political and religious events in the narrow sense. We can only speculate on the form Tacitus' historical work would have taken had he chosen to describe the slow transformations of intellectual life in Rome and of tribal life in the provinces.

Breaks of such far-reaching proportions were not unheard of in the world in which Tacitus lived. Christians and Cynics were prepared to leave behind them the forms and substance of Roman political life. The Christians had even invented new historiographical forms—the Gospels and the Acts of the Apostles—to express their new outlook. But Tacitus was neither a Christian nor a Cynic; and to be fair to him, neither the Christians nor the Cynics came near to asking the sort of questions we see implied in the *Germania* and in the dialogue *De Oratoribus*.

In short Tacitus did not pursue his most daring experiments, but devoted his major historical works to a subject which was less revolutionary without being conventional. He began to work in an analytical way on the most undesirable features of tyrannical government. The surviving part of the *Histories* is largely about civil war under tyrants, with its interconnected features of mob irresponsibility and upper-class greed for power. The *Annals* defy simple definition. Each emperor is analysed at his worst, his collaborators share his fate, and only a few individuals—mainly senators with a philosophical faith—escape condemnation because they face martyrdom.

A sober evaluation of the originality of such a historiographical enterprise is almost impossible. The evidence is missing. The works of Tacitus' predecessors are all lost. He may have learned something from Hellenistic historians who wrote chronicles of tyrants. The Athenian

Demochares, who in the first part of the third century B.C. gave a pas-
sionately hostile account of the government of Demetrius Poliorcetes in
Athens, certainly qualified as a model for antityrannical historians. But
tyranny in Greece was something provisional, something violently and
uneasily superimposed on a democratic structure. It seems highly unlikely that any Greek historian could really be of great use to a historian like Tacitus, who was describing the consequences of the permanent suppression of liberty. Tacitus was bound to learn much more
from his immediate predecessors, who were also his immediate
sources. Yet we must make a distinction between borrowing facts and
borrowing interpretations. I should be very embarrassed to assess the
originality of Tacitus as an interpreter of history on the present evidence. The comparison of Tacitus with Dio, Plutarch, and Suetonius is
conclusive about the existence of a common source for the facts, but is
quite inconclusive about the existence of a common source for the
interpretation of the facts. Yet where the comparison is easier, in
the *Histories*, the differences of interpretation between Tacitus and
the other surviving historians are conspicuous. Only Tacitus interprets
the crisis of 69 as the collapse of the discipline of the Roman army
made possible by the demoralisation of the Roman aristocracy. Neither Plutarch nor Dio interprets the events of 69 as the crisis of a society. When we read Tacitus, we immediately feel that he gives us
something different from the other historians. His analysis of human
behaviour is deeper, his attention to the social traditions, to the precise
circumstances, is far more vigorous. He conveys his interpretation by
a subtle and accurate choice of details which are expressed in an entirely personal language. The picture which sticks in our mind is his
own. To admit that Tacitus had real predecessors is to admit that there
was a Tacitean style before Tacitus. This is enough for our purpose, because ultimately our purpose is to show how his picture of despotism
became classic.

Tacitus' theoretical remarks on the beginning of the decline of
Rome, on the relative merits of fate and providence, and on the developments of political institutions are notoriously vague and even self-
contradictory. He consistently cared for the honour of Rome, for the
victory of its armies, for the extension of the borders of the Roman

State, even when he was clearly not certain about the merits of the Roman case. One of his accusations against Tiberius is that he was not interested in extending the Roman Empire (*Ann.* IV, 32). His accounts of wars are founded upon the presupposition that once a war was started the victory of Rome was automatically desirable. He took for granted the right of the Roman state to conquer and win—though he questioned the consequences. He liked fairness towards the provincials, but never doubted the right to repress any rebellion of the provincials. He extended his prejudice to include a great number of Roman upper-class likes and dislikes. Greeks, Jews, and Christians are looked down on, and there is the conventional contempt for *liberti* and more in general for mere plebeians. This means that the area in which he was prepared effectively to question the Roman imperial structure was limited. He had no ideas of his own about foreign policy, and in the matter of provincial policy he shared the widely felt opinion that the Latin West was more promising than the Greek East. The emperors of the first century A.D. very nearly practised what Tacitus preached about the rights of Rome, the policy of conquest, the dangers of aliens and mobs. On these points Tacitus' disagreement was marginal. His notoriously ambiguous account of the persecution of the Christians under Nero, though critical of the Emperor, does not question his ultimate right to persecute.

Tacitus' real aim was to unmask the imperial rule, in so far as it was government by debasement, hypocrisy, and cruelty. He did not exclude any class from the consequences of such a regime, but concentrated on the imperial court itself and on the senators. Individual exceptions he allowed. They were either the martyrs, like Thrasea Paetus, or the wise men, like Agricola, but it is characteristic of his more mature judgement that in the *Annals* the martyrs figure much more prominently than the wise men. To see the prostitution of the Roman aristocracy, to have to recognise that there was often more dignity in a German or British chieftain than in a Roman senator—that was the last bitterness of tyranny. The whole history of the years 68–70 is the consequence of the shameful weakness of the Roman Senate in changing masters five times. Nothing said against Tiberius equals the indictment of his Senate "pavor internus occupaverat animos, cui remedium adulatione quaerebatur" (IV, 74). *Adulatio* is the recurring word. Domitian's mind was corrupted by adulation: adulation is promised by Galba to Piso. On the other hand protests against the tyrant, if ever uttered, are not invariably praiseworthy: they run the risk of being useless and frivolous, *inane*. One of the aspects of tyranny is to impose a difficult choice between adulation and empty protest or, to put it in Tacitean words, "inter abruptam contumaciam et deforme obsequium" (*Ann.* IV, 20).

Such a situation, in which even the free word is only seldom appropriate, is the indication that something is radically wrong with human nature. Tyranny ceases to be an isolated phenomenon and becomes a symptom of a basic evil. Men are ready to forsake freedom for adulation—or to make fools of themselves by empty words of freedom. The more Tacitus pursues this point, from the *Histories* to the *Annals*, the more pessimistic he becomes. The deeper he looks, the more evident the contrast becomes between reality and appearances, between deeds and words in human behaviour. Yet, we must insist, Tacitus is no nihilist. His pessimism is perhaps more superficial than we are inclined to admit. Almost every story he tells us has a bad end, and he may give the impression that man cannot avoid going wrong. But there is much he does not tell us. What remains untold is safe enough. Family, property, rank, education on the whole do not seem to be in danger. Certainly Tacitus does not worry about them. Thucydides and Polybius registered much greater upheavals and were less querulous about them. Even power as such is not distrusted by Tacitus. He only dislikes tyrannical power.

Perhaps there is an insoluble conflict in Tacitus' approach to the Roman Empire. There is much that he approves of, so much, indeed, that he cannot criticise the institution as a whole. But he dislikes intensely the despotism which goes with it. Just because he cannot criticise the Empire as a whole, he comes to accept it as unmodifiable. And because he accepts it as unmodifiable, he cannot really see how it is possible to have an Empire without tyranny. He may have had hopes in that direction when he began to write the *Histories*, but those hopes had vanished long before he started the *Annals*. Thus he was led to admit an unchangeable element of evil in the Roman Empire. The psychology of the tyrant turned out to be only a prominent manifestation of the permanent greed, lust, and vanity of man as such. Paradoxically it is his conservatism which forces Tacitus to be a pessimist. He is a pessimist because he cannot even conceive of an alternative to the Roman Empire.

It is part of the insoluble conflict in Tacitus' mind that he never forgets that human nature is capable of true courage, true frankness, true liberty. Where so much adulation and hypocrisy prevail, he can give examples of freedom of speech. Furthermore, he envisages distant worlds where virtue could reign unimpaired: primitive Rome, or perhaps untouched barbarian lands. Admittedly these fairy lands are of limited practical importance. Tacitus makes it clear that any idea of a Roman republic in the old sense is by now obsolete and, with tragic irony, emphasises the danger that freedom-loving barbarians represent for the Roman State. But the individuals who at their own peril managed to keep alive the old freedom are of immense importance to Tacitus. He does not include himself among them. He never judges from the security of a morally superior position. One of his very rare personal notes is to confess that he had accepted Domitian's tyranny without offering resistance.

Tacitus had no intention of competing with the philosophers. He would have been very annoyed to be taken for one. Towards the greatest philosopher of the previous generation, Seneca, he maintained a guarded attitude. Modern scholars have been given plenty of scope to discuss whether Tacitus liked Seneca. His very admission of relative cowardice in the time of Domitian also serves the purpose of preventing any confusion between himself and the philosophers. He speaks from the middle of the Roman State and does not claim any exemption from its evils. Yet both the methods and the results of his historical writing recall the contemporary philosophers. He transferred to history the subtlety of analysis which philosophers had developed through the centuries of Hellenistic and Roman rule. He confirmed the opinion of those philosophers who thought that "virtus" was the rare achievement of individual effort, more often to be obtained by standing up against the government of the day than by governing others.

III

Tacitus' teaching about despotism was ambivalent. It was never meant to encourage revolutions, but would obviously open the eyes of anyone who cared to see the effects of despotism. Other people, however, could take it as an object lesson in the art of government, a lesson of realism.

In Antiquity few people were prepared to ponder such a complex message. A Tacitus could mature only in solitude. Even his contemporary Pliny the Younger, with all his admiration for Tacitus, was unable to grasp his friend's thought. Later Tacitus seems to have found a public among the last Romans of the fourth and fifth centuries. Ammianus Marcellinus sharpened his wits on Tacitus' pages. But nostalgia rather than ruthless objectivity was the keynote of the age: while Ammianus recaptured some of the spaciousness, nobility, and bitterness of the *Histories*, he no longer questioned human nature in the agonising way which is characteristic of Tacitus. Like El Greco many centuries later, Ammianus came to be interested in the world (visually) because it appeared ill-proportioned and quaint. Other aristocrats with learned tastes, especially in Gaul, enjoyed their Tacitus without further probing into his teaching. There was a friend of Sidonius Apollinaris who even claimed descent from Tacitus (*Ep.* IV, 14); Sulpicius Severus and Orosius used him extensively. People went on quoting him in the sixth century. But he must by then have been a very dim figure if Cassiodorus, who used his *Germania*, could refer to him as a "certain Cornelius," "Cornelio quodam" (*Variae* V, 2).

During the Middle Ages, only a few read Tacitus, and almost all of them were in Benedictine monasteries either in Germany (such as Fulda) or connected with Germany (such as Montecassino). Our most important manuscript of the later part of the *Annals* and of the *Histories* (the *Mediceus secundus* in the Laurentian Library) was apparently stolen from Montecassino in the fourteenth century. The story that Boccaccio was the thief has unfortunately proved to be unreliable. The Minor Works were brought from Germany to Italy in the fifteenth century: here again the details are notoriously uncertain, but the Minor Works were in Rome by about 1455. For the rest of the century there was no further increase in the knowledge of Tacitus' text; but what people had was enough to make minds work. Florence was the first intellectual and political centre to react to Tacitus' message, just as it was the first to appreciate Polybius. Characteristically Leonardo Bruni used Polybius to supplement Livy for the story of Roman wars and extracted from Tacitus the notion that great intellects vanish when all power is concentrated in one man. Bruni's quotation of Tacitus in his *Laudatio Florentinae Urbis* (of about 1403)—"Nam posteaquam res publica in unius potestatem deducta est, preclara illa ingenia (ut inquit Cornelius) abiere"—is the first evidence for the appearance of Tacitus in modern political thought. About thirty years later Poggio Bracciolini turned to Tacitus again to support, against Guarino Guarini, the superiority of republican Scipio over monarchic Caesar. This, however, was a use of Tacitus which derived its significance from the special position of Florence in its struggle against Milan ruled by the Visconti, and lost importance with the general decline of republican ideals in Florence itself and in the rest of Italy. Furthermore, the Florentine interpretation of what was known of Tacitus did not provide a clue to the understanding of the only conspicuous exception in this decline—the republic of Venice.

As far as I know (but I am not a specialist in the political literature of the Quattrocento), Tacitus was put aside in Italy about 1440 for a good sixty years. These are the years in which the Germans were learning to read the *Germania*. Enea Silvio Piccolomini first brought it to the attention of the Germans in 1458. By 1500 it had become a mirror in which the Germans liked to look at themselves. Conrad Celtis was apparently the first to lecture on Tacitus in a German university, in about 1492. He started the tradition of investigation into German antiquities which his pupil Johannes Aventinus, together with Beatus Rhenanus, Sebastian Münster, and many others, was to continue. The learned enquiry both implied and fostered a claim of independence and perhaps of superiority in relation to the imperial Rome of the past and the papal Rome of the present. Tacitus was beginning to repay the hospitality he had received in German monasteries during the Middle Ages.

At this point the manuscript of Books I–VI of the *Annals*, according to contemporary evidence, was stolen from Corvey and brought to Rome about 1509. There seems to be no serious reason to doubt this story. Philippus Beroaldus published the *editio princeps* of the first books of the *Annals* in 1515. Tiberius' ghost was returning at the right time. Machiavelli had written *Il Principe* two years before. He was working at the same time on those *Discorsi sulla Prima Deca* which destroyed any illusion the Florentines might ever have had about the similarity of their government with that of republican Rome.

Tiberius was accompanied by another no less timely ghost, that of Arminius "liberator haud dubie Germaniae." Almost on the heels of Beroaldus' edition Ulrich von Hutten wrote the *Arminius dialogus* (c. 1520), a momentous event in the history of German nationalism. Tacitus is called in as witness by Arminius and is asked to recite "elogium illud meum quod in historiis tuis est." In the *Ragguagli del Parnaso* by Traiano Boccalini the reactionary god Apollo puts together Luther and the manuscript of Tacitus as the two worst things which had ever come out of Germany. Tacitus found himself at the confluence of the two great movements of the sixteenth century, religious reform and monarchic absolutism. In the later *Discorsi*, Machiavelli himself quoted little of Tacitus and almost nothing of the newly discovered section on Tiberius. His few quotations, however, showed something of more general importance than his obvious sympathy for Tacitus. They showed that Tacitus' books made sense only if used to explain why even republican Rome—for all her ability to turn political struggles into sources of political strength—fell under the control of monarchs. Tacitus was the complement to Livy—the historian who more than Tacitus had been the guide of earlier humanistic historians. Guicciardini with his talent for the right word produced the formula for the new movement of ideas: "Tacitus teaches the tyrants how to be tyrants and their subjects how to behave under tyrants." The ambivalence of Tacitus is here recognised—perhaps for the first time. It is this ambivalence that explains why he might alternatively serve the purposes of the friends and of the enemies of absolutism. Cosimo I Medici and Pope Paul III Farnese were among the most diligent readers of Tacitus. It has even been suggested that the Medici and the Farnese as family groups became special devotees of Tacitus.

There were resistances to be overcome before Tacitus could be accepted as a major teacher of political wisdom. The truest classicists stuck to Cicero and Livy. The pious remembered that Tacitus had been attacked by Tertullian (*Ad Nat.* I, 11) for his pages on the Christians. Budé could not forgive Tacitus on grounds of religion: "Hominem nefarium Tacitum. . . ." The circumstance that another dubious character, Jean Bodin, took up the case of Tacitus against Budé was perhaps not a recommendation. Only when the split between Catholic and Protestant Europe became an accepted fact—and theological disputes lost something of their urgency—did Tacitus gain full authority. We may put the turning point around 1580, when Marc-Antoine Muret started to give lectures on Tacitus' *Annals* at the University of Rome—the very centre of the Counter-Reformation. Tacitus was both the exegete and the critic of political absolutism: the ambiguity pleased almost everyone. He helped the new search into the obscurities of the human soul. Montaigne studied and admired him, and all the later French moralists from Charron to La Rochefoucauld owed something to him, especially in the study of hypocrisy. Modern Dutch literature was almost brought to life by the contact of Dutch intellectuals with Tacitus. Two other factors contributed. The condemnation of Machiavelli's works by the Catholic Church (1559) had left an empty space which Tacitus could easily fill. What could not be said in the name of Catholic Machiavelli could be said in the name of pagan Tacitus. If somebody objected to Tacitus, one could always reply that a pagan was not supposed to know the whole truth. Second, Ciceronianism was undergoing a crisis. The popularity of Seneca both as a stylist and as a philosopher was mounting; Neo-Stoicism became the faith of those who had lost patience with theology, if they had not lost faith altogether. The fortunes of Seneca and Tacitus became indissolubly connected towards the end of the sixteenth century. In the controversy between the Italians and the French about the superiority of their respective languages, the ability to translate Tacitus became a test case. As is well known, Davanzati's translation of Tacitus was the answer to some derogatory remarks by Henricus Stephanus. Davanzati tried to prove that one could write as concisely in Italian as Tacitus had done in Latin. Davanzati was successful in writing short sentences, but Italian remained a language of interminable sentences. One man represented the new synthesis of Seneca and Tacitus: Muret's disciple, Justus Lipsius. If his mind was more with Seneca, his heart, his personal experience, were for Tacitus. Justus Lipsius loved Tacitus so much, interpreted him so learnedly, pressed his case so authoritatively, and combined his teaching with that of Seneca so ingeniously that it was impossible not to listen to him. Because Justus Lipsius, who was born a Catholic and ended a Catholic, spent part of his learned life in the Protestant camp, he made propaganda for Tacitus on both sides of the fence. His contemporaries regarded Lipsius as the real discoverer of Tacitus, and they were substantially right. But I was able to show many years ago (*Contributo*, pp. 37–59) that another current of thought contributed to the same result. The study of Tacitus as a political thinker was introduced in Paris by an Italian emigré, who like Lipsius wavered between Protestantism and Catholicism, Carolus Paschalius, or Carlo Pasquale. Both Paschalius and Lipsius published a commentary on Tacitus in 1581. But whereas Lipsius was chiefly interested in illustrating the historical allusions in Tacitus and in interpreting his words, Paschalius treated Tacitus as a collection of political *exampla*. Lipsius availed himself of Tacitus as a political thinker only in 1589, when he published his *Politicorum libri VI*, but not even then did he use Tacitus so extensively, indeed exclusively, as Paschalius had done in his commentary of 1581. Though all the later Tacitisti, as they were called, were encouraged by the authority of Justus Lipsius, they depended more directly on Carolus Paschalius for the type of their enquiry and for the form of presentation. The rapid progress of Tacitus' reputation as a political thinker in those years can be shown by this significant chronological sequence. The Jesuit Giovanni Botero did not yet know of Tacitus as an important political thinker when he wrote his *De Regia Sapientia* in 1582. In 1589, when he published his *Ragion di Stato*, after a stay in Paris, he put together Machiavelli and Tacitus as the leading writers on politics.

The commentaries and dissertations on Tacitus of the next hundred years are innumerable; Machiavellian Italy led the Tacitist movement, and Spain, France, and Germany followed—I venture to believe—in this order. England contributed comparatively little, and Holland too was not conspicuous in this type of production. England and Holland were the countries which were to give Europe her modern political thought with Hobbes, Grotius, Spinoza, and Locke. The defeat of the Armada saved England, among other things, from being invaded by Tacitus, or by the Tacitisti. But if Ben Jonson got into trouble for his *Sejanus* in 1603, some connection with the mounting wave of the Tacitism of those years must be admitted. Ben Jonson himself had greeted Sir Henry Savile's translation and supplementation of the *Histories* in 1591 by an epigram (no. 95) which is an interesting characterisation of Tacitus from the Tacitist point of view:

> We need a man, can speake of the intents,
> The councells, actions, orders and events
> Of state, and censure them: we need his pen
> Can write the things, the causes, and the men.

Books of foreign Tacitists were translated into English—Boccalini, Virgilio Malvezzi. Others were read in the original or in Latin translations. What is perhaps true is that in England there was a tendency to emphasise the antityrannical aspects of Tacitus. Bacon took him for an enemy of absolute monarchy. The Dutch Dr. Isaac Dorislaus, who became the first holder of a lectureship in History at Cambridge in 1627, had soon to leave his chair because he interpreted Tacitus in an obviously antimonarchical spirit. Ultimately, however, in England the most serious thinkers worried about the divine rights of kings, not about the psychology of tyranny. As the dispute between Salmasius and Milton shows in an exemplary way, biblical texts counted for more than Tacitus.

The Tacitist literature of the Continent can be divided into four groups: (1) Excerpts from Tacitus in the form of political aphorisms. For instance, Abraham Gölnitz in his *Princeps* of 1636 describes what a prince must do in peace and war by means of excerpts from Tacitus. (2) Excerpts from Tacitus accompanied by a detailed political commentary: Virgilio Malvezzi's *Discorsi* are a good sample. They belong to what Bacon would have called "historiae ruminatae." (3) General theories on politics vaguely founded on Tacitus, such as the *Quaestiones ac Discursus in duos primos libros Annalium* by Petrus Andreas

Canonherius (Canoniero). (4) Political commentaries on Tacitus, which wavered somewhat ambiguously between an analysis of Tacitus' opinions and an analysis of the facts related by Tacitus. The commentaries by Annibale Scoto and by Traiano Boccalini are of this type.

Tacitus became fashionable. He was even put into Italian verse by Alessandro Adimari, *La Polinnia, ovvero cinquanta sonetti . . . fondati sopra sentenze di G. Cornelio Tacito*, 1628. Like every other fashion "Tacitismo" became tiresome after a time and found itself in conflict with more modern trends. As I have already implied, doubts on Tacitus had always been maintained in certain Catholic circles. The Spanish Jesuit Pedro Ribadeneira put together in one bunch Tiberius, "a very vicious and abominable emperor," Tacitus, "a pagan historian and enemy of Christianity," Machiavelli, "the impious counsellor," and Bodin, who "was neither learned in theology nor accustomed to piety." The other Jesuit authority on Machiavelli, Antonio Possevino, complained that too many of his contemporaries seemed to forget that one syllable of the Gospel is preferable to the whole of Tacitus. And in 1617 Famiano Strada, better known to the English for his influence on Richard Crashaw's poetry, published a determined attack on Tacitus. He renewed the accusation of atheism and also tried to revive, against Tacitus, the declining cult for Livy. The fact that Spinoza liked Tacitus for his anti-Jewish and anti-Christian bias did not improve the pagan author's popularity in pious circles.

About a century later dislike for Tacitus was expressed both on the right and on the left, by Catholics and by rationalists. While he was too much of a pagan for the Catholics, the libertines and rationalists disliked him for being too cynical and anyway too clearly connected with the Counter-Reformation. The decline of Spanish supremacy in Europe, the ascendancy of England and the Netherlands, the rise of Cartesian rationalism and of Jansenism in France, were destroying the presuppositions upon which Tacitus had gained his authority. For once Fénélon and Bayle found themselves in agreement on the point that Tacitus defeated his own purposes by too much subtlety: "il a trop d'esprit, il rapine trop." Saint-Évremond complained that Tacitus turned everything into politics: Voltaire himself had no use for Tacitus, who, according to the *Traité sur la Tolérance*, preferred slander to truth. In a letter to Madame du Deffand (no. 14202), Voltaire explained that Tacitus did not comply with the new standards of a History of Civilisation: "I (Voltaire) should like to know the rights of the Senate, the forces of the empire, the number of the citizens, the form of government, the customs, the habits. I do not find anything of the sort in Tacitus. *Il m'amuse, et Tite-Live m'instruit.*" People interested in the new idea of parliamentary government spreading from England found Tacitus less instructive than the historians of the Roman Republic, such as Polybius and Livy. On the other hand the supporters of Continental enlightened despotism discovered that Tacitus was an embarrassment to their cause: his emperors were only too clearly unenlightened despots.

This might well have been the end of the Tacitist period in modern political thought if Tacitus had not found new allies in unexpected circles. To begin with, Giambattista Vico recognised in Tacitus one of his four guides to the discovery of the laws of history. He was interested in Tacitus as the student of primitive, violent impulses—a complement to Plato. Following a suggestion by Francis Bacon (*De augmentis scientiarum*, 7, 2), Vico regarded Tacitus as the portrayer of man as he is, while Plato contemplates man as he should be. Vico revalued Tacitus and Machiavelli, as it were, from a higher point of view. The same was done—independently and more crudely, but with greater consequences—by the French Encyclopaedists. Machiavelli was rescued by the French Encyclopaedists partly because his works had been put on the Index, partly because they adopted the old extreme Baconian interpretation that he was secretly hitting at despotism. Rousseau produced the new formula in the *Contrat Social* (ch. VI): "The Prince of Machiavelli is the book of the Republicans." What was good for Machiavelli was even better for Tacitus. D'Alembert, who wrote the article on Machiavellianism in the *Encyclopédie*, also published an anthology of Tacitus. Rousseau, too, translated some Tacitus. They turned Tacitus into an enlightened enemy of obscurantist princes. This is the Tacitus, wise and mild, who prevailed in Europe immediately before the French Revolution. We recognise him in Gibbon's definition of Tacitus as "the first of historians who applied the science of philosophy to the study of facts" (*Decline and Fall*, ed. Bury, ch. IX, p. 230). Gibbon learned

more than one stylistic trick from Tacitus. With due acknowledgement
to d'Alembert and Gibbon, John Hill treated him in a similar way in
a really important paper published in the Transactions of the Royal
Academy of Edinburgh in 1788. But in England the interpretation inspired by the French Encyclopaedists had been somewhat anticipated
in 1728 by Walpole's friend Thomas Gordon, the "snoring Silenus" of
the second *Dunciad*. Gordon was an "unsparing critic of the priest-
hood." He compared Tacitus with St. Jerome to the advantage of the
former: "in Tacitus you have the good sense and breeding of a Gentle-
man; in the Saint the rage and dreams of a Monk" (Discourse II in *The
Works of Tacitus*, I, 1, p. 49). I suspect that when in 1752 the Reverend
Thomas Hunter published his *Observations on Tacitus. In which his
character as a writer and an historian, is impartially considered, and
compared with that of Livy* he was hitting at Gordon as much as at
Tacitus. It is no wonder that Gordon found a French publisher during
the Revolution.

Meanwhile the enlightened Tacitus of d'Alembert and Gibbon had
advanced further and had turned into a revolutionary republican: "Et
son nom prononcé fait pâlir les tyrans" (M.-J. Chénier, *Epître à Voltaire*, 1806). He was a republican to be used against tyrannies of every
kind. Camille Desmoulins quoted Tacitus—or rather, Gordon's Tacitus—against Robespierre in the pages of his *Vieux Cordelier*. Vittorio
Alfieri fed on Tacitus' works, and in Foscolo's juvenile novel the hero,
Jacopo Ortis, equally hostile to monarchic and to democratic terror,
commits suicide after having translated "the whole second book of the
Annals and the greater part of the second of the Histories." The mere
name of Tacitus made Napoleon I angry. We could tell a long story
about the part played by Tacitus in the struggle against the Caesarism
of both Napoleons. French intellectuals were divided between those
who admired Caesar and those who admired Tacitus. The Bonapartist
Revue Contemporaine was definitely against Tacitus. The *Revue des
Deux Mondes* can approximately be described as pro-Tacitus. Gaston
Boissier, who wrote the best book on Tacitus of the nineteenth century,
was a contributor to the *Revue des Deux Mondes*.

The battle over French Caesarism—and the word Caesarism was invented by Auguste Romieu in 1850—was the last episode of modern

political life in which Tacitus played a direct, unsophisticated role. This is not to deny that in even more recent times—for instance, during Fascism or the Vichy régime—books on Tacitus were inspired by modern political passions. Concetto Marchesi's well-known book on Tacitus, for instance, was written in hatred of Fascism (1924). But in the course of the nineteenth century it became increasingly difficult to talk about modern problems as if they were Roman ones. The French battle about Caesarism closed an epoch—which had started at the beginning of the sixteenth century.

For three centuries Tacitus taught modern readers what tyranny is. No doubt there were philosophers and moralists, from Plato to Epictetus, who had something very important to convey on the same subject. But philosophers talk in abstract terms. Tacitus portrayed individuals. He was so lucid, so memorable, that no philosopher could compete with him. It was Tacitus who transmitted the ancient experience of tyranny to modern readers. Other historians and biographers—such as Diodorus, Suetonius, and Plutarch—were far less authoritative: they had been unable to produce a convincing life-size picture of a despot. Thucydides, Xenophon, Polybius, Livy, Sallust, competed with each other for the attention of the modern reader in the matter of republican government. Tacitus on despotism was left without rival. True, at least in the sixteenth and seventeenth centuries the image of the Tacitean despot was reproduced for the benefit of the modern reader in works of political theory rather than in books of history. I have already explained why this is perhaps not surprising. It was the essence of Tacitism to furnish indirectly that analysis of the political contemporary situation which it would have been technically difficult—and perhaps also more politically dangerous—to formulate in plain historical works. But this is perhaps the moment to add that the historiography of these two centuries is insufficiently explored, and studies on the imitation of ancient models are needed especially. Mariana, John Hayward, William Camden, Grotius, Davila, and later Johannes Müller are names that immediately come to mind as historians who admired and imitated Tacitus. How much do we know about the exact forms of this imitation? Similarly I do not know of an adequate study of A.-N. Amelot de La Houssaye, the greatest Tacitist of France and the translator of Baltasar Gracián, who was also the writer of the *Histoire du Gouvernement de Venise* (1676), a classic in the interpretation of the Venetian constitution. Even in the early nineteenth century there are still historians who stylistically and psychologically imitate Tacitus in a way requiring some explanation. Such are the three most important Italian historians of that time, Carlo Botta, Pietro Colletta, and Carlo Troya. Indeed it is impossible to describe Italian historiography of the early nineteenth century without reference to Tacitus. The influence of Tacitus as a historian was inherent in his authority as a source for the history of the Roman Empire. Every educated man read Tacitus, accepted his picture of Tiberius and Nero, and learned from it how to understand the psychology of tyranny.

It is not difficult to see why such a situation should change in the nineteenth century, and why the change first became apparent in Germany. The Romantic revolution gave preference to those historians who expressed conflicts of ideas rather than conflicts of personalities. To be called a pragmatic historian became a term of abuse in certain circles. At the very beginning of the nineteenth century Schelling declared that Herodotus and Thucydides were to be preferred to Polybius and Tacitus. At least as far as Thucydides was concerned, his judgement was generally accepted. Later, under the guidance of Mommsen, the studies on the Roman Empire were increasingly directed towards the provinces, the army, the administration—all subjects to which Tacitus could contribute less than the *Corpus Inscriptionum Latinarum.* Tacitus was declared to be the least military of the historians and was accused of being badly informed about Roman provincial administration. It was also shown that he followed his sources very closely— which seemed to cast a shadow on his competence as a historian. All the basic criticisms were made or at least confirmed by Mommsen. In a famous memoir of 1870 he opened a new phase in the analysis of the sources of Tacitus. He himself refrained from any derogatory remark and always respected Tacitus' judgement of life under the emperors. The definition of Tacitus as a monarchist from despair comes from him. Mommsen himself was a pessimistic supporter of the German Empire. But scholars who followed Mommsen too narrowly were bound to dislike or to underrate Tacitus.

Admirers of Tacitus had to try various lines of defence. Some did their best to cover him by pointing out that he was not a pragmatic historian, but an artist. This was a valid defence against Schelling's criticism because Schelling put art—"Kunst"—above everything else. In this sense J. W. Süvern wrote his famous paper *Ueber den Kunstcharakter des Tacitus*, published by the Berlin Academy in 1823. Other students of historiography suggested that Polybius and Tacitus were nearer than Herodotus and Thucydides to Christian truth and were therefore to be preferred. But the definition of Tacitus as an artist could easily turn into an admission that he was not a historian. At the end of the century Friedrich Leo, who owed so much to Mommsen, proclaimed Tacitus a poet, one of the few great poets Rome had ever had, only to damn him as a historian. Few or none of those people who defended Tacitus in Germany were so bold or so naive as to say that Tacitus was true, as French scholars still did. Finally, the negative appreciation of Tacitus prevailed everywhere, even in France, where he had found his steadiest admirers, as the works by Ph. Fabia and E. Courbaud showed.

Today we can see the point of these nineteenth-century discussions about the merits of Tacitus without having to agree. The dispute about Tacitus has definitely passed to another stage. Tacitus has his own obvious limits. Within these limits there can be no doubt on our part that he saw something essential: the demoralisation that goes together with despotism. Mussolini and Hitler and Stalin have done something for his reputation. Furthermore, we cannot now judge an ancient writer without asking ourselves what he represented in the history of mediaeval and modern humanism. The transition from the Roman Republic to the Roman Principate remains to the present day a problem of immediate relevance to us. This would never have happened without Tacitus. He is our master in the study of despotism. His methods can be applied, and have been applied, to other periods. His analysis of human motives has been discussed, and often accepted, by the leading moralists of the last centuries. But there is perhaps something even simpler and more immediate to be said about Tacitus. He was interested in individual men and women. He went beyond appearances and made an effort to interpret their minds. He wrote as a man who was inside the process of tyrannical corruption which he was describing. He makes us realise that we, too, are inside.

CHAPTER SIX

The Origins of
Ecclesiastical Historiography

I

The connection between ecclesiastical history and fireworks is perhaps not the most obvious. But at least in one case fireworks demonstrably helped the study of ecclesiastical history. The name of Benedetto Bacchini stands out among the learned Benedictine monks of the end of the seventeenth century. Born in Parma in 1661, he was the first Italian to apply the methods of research on mediaeval history which Mabillon had made authoritative in France. But there was much distrust of Bacchini's work in both the ecclesiastical and the courtly circles of Parma and Modena where he worked, and his character did not make things easier. He had, however, one asset which was of course not so uncommon among seventeenth-century scholars as it is now: he knew engineering and chemistry. This enabled him to preside successfully over the preparations for the fireworks to celebrate the wedding of Rinaldo d'Este Duke of Modena in 1696. The Duke was pleased; and as a result Bacchini was asked in 1697 to take charge of the Ducal Library, which, like many other Italian libraries, had been sadly neglected in the previous century. His commission only lasted a little more than a year. The journal which he edited and indeed wrote almost single-handed, *Il Giornale dei Letterati*, incurred the Inquisition's displeasure with its defence of the Bollandist Papebrochius. The *Giornale* was soon stopped, and Bacchini was ordered to go back to his monastery as *cellerarius*—the bursar. Not even Montfaucon, who was in Italy at the time, could save him from this rather uncongenial task. But the one year during which Bacchini was free to examine the manuscripts of the Ducal Library was sufficient for the discovery with which Bacchini's name is connected forever—the discovery of the *Liber Pontificalis* of Agnellus of Ravenna. It was really a rediscovery. The ninth-century chronicle of the Bishopric of Ravenna had been read in Ravenna itself by learned humanists of the fifteenth and sixteenth centuries, such as Flavio Biondo and Giovanni Pietro Ferretti. But the later and most important historian of Ravenna, Hieronymus Rubaeus or Gerolamo Rossi, who wrote about 1590, was unable to consult it and complained that it had disappeared from the Bishop's library. The copy which Bacchini found in Modena in 1697 does not seem to have been that which had disappeared from Ravenna before 1590. It was a manuscript of the fifteenth century. The chronicle of Agnellus was still a very controversial document several centuries after its compilation. So controversial was its character that this probably explains why it was taken away from Ravenna in the sixteenth century. It was certainly to cause Bacchini many troubles when he tried to publish it about 1705.

The author of the chronicle, Agnellus, a priest in Ravenna between circa 820 and 845, compiled his *Liber Pontificalis* as a series of lectures for his fellow priests of the Capitolum of Ravenna. Though he lived at a time when the see of Ravenna had become reconciled to subordination to Rome, he felt plainly nostalgic for those proud days in which the Archbishop of Ravenna with the help of Byzantium had defied Rome and claimed total independence, *autokephalia*. He tells with obvious relish how Archbishop Maurus died in 671 after having advised his successors never to accept the insignia of their dignity—the pallium—from Rome: "Pallium ab imperatore petite, quacumque enim die Romae subiugati fueritis, non eritis integri. Et his dictis obiit" (*P. L.* 106, col. 673).

One of Agnellus' allegations was particularly serious and could not be overlooked in any ecclesiastical controversy. He stated that in the early fifth century the Emperor Valentinianus III had granted the Bishop of Ravenna the rank of Archbishop and had consequently given him the pallium. As we all know, the right to confer the pallium is one of the most jealously defended prerogatives of the Pope of Rome: no Archbishop is considered to be in legitimate possession of his see unless he has asked for, and obtained from the Pope, the insignia of the pallium. A practice going back perhaps to the fourth century and a theory certainly well established by the eighth century invested the pallium with a transcendental meaning and made it a symbol of papal authority over the other metropolitan churches. Both theory and practice of the conferment of the pallium had been the subject of controversy since the time of the Reformation, and doubts about the exclusive right of the Pope to grant the pallium had been expressed not only by non-Catholics but also by the supporters of the Gallican movement within the Catholic Church. Any text purporting to show that between the fourth and the sixth century of Christianity the emperor had conferred the pallium upon a bishop was consequently bound to rouse passions on every side. It might set a dangerous precedent even in the seventeenth century. Well before Bacchini's rediscovery of Agnellus other authentic cases of conferment of the pallium by Roman and early Byzantine emperors had already been noted and collected by religious controversialists of the seventeenth century. The most formidable case for the right of an emperor or king to grant the pallium to the bishops of his own territory had been stated by the Parisian Archbishop Pierre de Marca: and forty years after its posthumous appearance in 1669 de Marca's work was still at the centre of the controversy about the rights of Rome over the French Church.

To complicate matters, Agnellus' was not the only evidence for the alleged conferment of the pallium on the Bishop of Ravenna by the Roman Emperor Valentinianus. A document circulating in the fifteenth and sixteenth centuries claimed to be the text of the grant by Valentinian III to Bishop John of Ravenna. But Baronius had had no difficulty in proving that this was a forged document. Although some obdurate opponents of the rights of Rome—such as A. M. De Dominis—were unwilling to take notice of Baronius' exposure, the most serious scholars of the seventeenth century—on both sides—had all accepted his findings. The question was reopened, however, when Bacchini drew attention to the statement by Agnellus in the *Liber Pontificalis*, thus implying that tradition lent some support to the forged document. Here was a historian of the ninth century, demonstrably independent of the forged document, who yet maintained with precise details that a Roman Emperor—not a Roman Pope—had conferred the pallium on the Bishop of Ravenna. The statement was the more impressive because Agnellus, for all his partisan views, was clearly a very learned man: he had a habit of quoting documents, of using pictures and inscriptions to support his facts, which could not but impress a world of antiquarians such as that in which Bacchini lived.

Bacchini himself was on the whole a keen supporter of the Church of Rome and had no wish to scandalise his readers. But he was not the man to dismiss a piece of evidence because it was inconvenient, and as a follower of the Maurists he was ready to admit a certain amount of evolution in the development of Christian institutions. A few years later, in 1724, the posthumous work on the history of the pallium by the Maurist Dom Thierry Ruinart was published—one of the masterpieces of the Benedictine school, in which the same point of view is expressed. But of course Bacchini could not have known this as yet. In his heart Bacchini really could not feel that there was anything reprehensible in the Emperor Valentinian's having conferred metropolitan rights on the Bishop of Ravenna. This is not to say that he was prepared to accept Agnellus' statement about Valentinian III: even now it is impossible to say whether Agnellus is correct. But Bacchini was obviously in two minds about the origins of the Archbishopric of Ravenna, and his doubts went so far as to involve the whole history of the metropolitan sees in the first centuries of the Church. He could not share the prevailing view that the organisation of the Church reflected the organisation of the Roman Empire. His book of 1703 on the origins of the ecclesiastical hierarchy, in which he formulated an alternative theory, caused some dissent but was allowed to pass. The edition of Agnellus Ravennas with introduction and commentary which he submitted to the ecclesiastical authorities in 1705 met with definite disapproval. At a certain point the Inquisition intervened and requested Bacchini to surrender all his papers on Agnellus: at the same time the Librarian of the Duke of Modena, L. A. Muratori, who was Bacchini's pupil, was asked not to allow outsiders to read the *Liber Pontificalis* of Ravenna. Finally, a compromise was reached. Bacchini consented to write a new preface in which he had to declare that Agnellus' statement on the pallium was utterly incredible and wicked—

and after many further negotiations about details the *Liber Pontificalis* could appear in 1708. It was incidentally the last book Bacchini was permitted to publish. At least two others were stopped by censorship.

I have dwelt on this episode not only because it is little known, but also because I feel it serves to bring home most immediately one of the distinctive features of ecclesiastical history—and consequently of ecclesiastical historiography. An event of the fifth century as told by a local ecclesiastical historian of the ninth century still had practical implications for the eighteenth century—and not only in Ravenna, but everywhere in Christendom. Both the continuity of Church history and the interrelation between local events and general principles of Church life are illustrated in our episode. Precedents of course matter in any kind of history—and there is nothing in the past that in certain circumstances cannot provoke passions in the present. We have had the language of the Macedonians about 350 B.C. or the evacuation of Roman Dacia in A.D. 270 debated by our own contemporaries as if they were questions of life or death for a modern state. But in no other history does precedent mean so much as in ecclesiastical history. The very continuity of the institution of the Church through the centuries makes it inevitable that anything which happened in the Church's past should be relevant to its present. Furthermore—and this is most essential—in the Church conformity with the origins is evidence of truth. This doctrine may be interpreted differently in the various denominations; but it is never absent in any of them. A Church that consciously breaks with its original principles and its original institutions is inconceivable. The Church knows a return to the principles, not a break with the principles. This in a sense simplifies the task of the Church historian. He has to write the history of an institution which began in a precise moment, had an original structure, and developed with clear changes. It is for him to judge where the change implies a betrayal of the original purposes of the institution. On the other hand the historian of the Church is inevitably faced with the difficulty of having continuously to relate the events of individual local churches to the *corpus mysticum* of the *Ecclesia universalis*. From this follow certain consequences for the methods of writing ecclesiastical history. Other historians can be satisfied with simply retelling the past. The chances that they will be challenged are few. The historian of the Church knows that at any point he will be challenged. The questions with which he deals are controversial. And the controversy is never one of pure dogma or of pure fact—the two are interrelated. The question of the granting of the pallium by Valentinian III—to return to our case—was one of both fact and theory. Any ecclesiastical historian who believes in Christianity is bound also to be a theologian. But if he is challenged on facts, he *must* produce evidence. What is unmistakably apparent in ecclesiastical historians is the care for their documentation.

Plenty of documents are already to be found in the earliest ecclesiastical historians—Eusebius, Socrates, Sozomenus, Theodoretus: they had adopted the scholarly habits of the Alexandrian antiquarians and grammarians. They are properly described by Sozomenus: "I have sought for records of events of earlier date amongst the established laws appertaining to religion, amongst the proceedings of the synods of the period, amongst the novelties that arose, and in the epistles of kings and priests. Some of these documents are preserved in palaces and churches, and others are dispersed, and in the possession of the learned. I thought seriously, at one time, of transcribing the whole, but on further reflection I deemed it better, on account of the prolixity of the documents, to give merely a brief synopsis of their contents" (Book I, 1, transl. E. Walford, London, 1855, p. 11). Socrates prepared a second edition of the first books of his Ecclesiastical History when he discovered texts of Athanasius, who contradicted his previous source, Rufinus. For the moment it is enough to remind ourselves that the very importance of precedent and tradition in ecclesiastical history compelled the ecclesiastical historians to quote documentary evidence to an extent which is seldom to be found in political historians.

Further research will have to establish where Agnellus found inspiration for his extensive use of literary and archaeological evidence. But even in the ninth century his is not an isolated case of care for documentation. Anastasius Bibliothecarius' contributions to the Roman *Liber Pontificalis* are supported by his minute knowledge of the papal archives. In the tenth century Flodoard of Rheims, the author of the *Historia Remensis ecclesiae*, was a formidable *érudit*: he seems to have undertaken a journey from Rheims to Rome to collect documents.

About 1080 Adam of Bremen used an extraordinary quantity of original documents and excerpts from earlier chronicles in his *Gesta Hammaburgensis ecclesiae pontificum*. Later in the twelfth century William of Malmesbury displayed antiquarian learning in his *On the Antiquity of the Church of Glastonbury*. John of Salisbury in his *Historia Pontificalis* proves to be an expert critic of the authenticity of papal rescripts (ch. 43).

We have defined what seem to us some of the essential elements of ecclesiastical historiography: the continuous interrelation of dogma and facts; the transcendental significance attributed to the period of the origins; the emphasis on factual evidence; the ever present problem of relating events of local churches to the mystical body of the Universal Church. But with this we have done little more than to define some of the features of the first ecclesiastical history—the Ecclesiastical History of Eusebius of Caesarea. In so far as Eusebius of Caesarea was the first to write a history of the Church from the point of view of the believer, he opened a new period in the history of historiography. Indeed one may doubt whether any other ancient historian made such an impact on successive generations as he did. The men who followed him shared his faith in the Church—and this created a bond that no pagan historian could establish with his Christian followers, nor indeed with his pagan colleagues.

II

Simple and majestic Eusebius of Caesarea claims for himself the merit of having invented ecclesiastical history. This merit cannot be disputed. The search for Eusebius' precursors started very early: it had been begun, perhaps not surprisingly, by one of his immediate continuators, Sozomenus. Sozomenus thought that Eusebius had been preceded as an ecclesiastical historian by Clemens, Hegesippus, and Julius Africanus. None of these names can really compete with that of Eusebius. The Clemens to whom Sozomenus alluded was the alleged author of the Gospel of Peter—not an ecclesiastical history; Sextus Julius Africanus is the well-known chronographer; and the more mysterious Hegesippus—quoted by Eusebius himself—does not seem to have written an ecclesiastical history at all: from the fragments he appears to have been an anti-Gnostic apologist of the second century A.D. Eusebius defines the purpose of his work in the opening paragraph: "I have purposed to record in writing the successions of the sacred apostles covering the period stretching from our Saviour to ourselves; the number and character of the transactions recorded in the history of the Church; the number of those who were distinguished in her government . . . ; the number of those who in each generation were the ambassadors of the word of God either by speech or pen; the names, the number and the age of those who, driven by the desire of innovation to an extremity of error, have heralded themselves as the introducers of Knowledge, falsely so called. To this I will add the fate which has beset the whole nation of the Jews . . . moreover the number and nature and times of the wars waged by the heathen against the divine word . . . furthermore the martyrdoms" (Loeb). In a sense Eusebius was the most unlikely person to have invented ecclesiastical history. His other masterpiece, *Praeparatio evangelica*, is one of the boldest attempts ever made to show continuity between pagan and Christian thought. We should hardly expect the same man to want to cut history into two parts—one devoted to the wordly affairs of war and politics, the other to the origin and development of the Christian Church. But the witness of the last persecution and the adviser and apologist of Constantine was in a vantage position to appreciate the autonomy and strength of the institution that had compelled the Roman state to surrender at the Milvian Bridge in 312. Though anxious to preserve the pagan cultural heritage in the new Christian order—indeed very anxious, as we shall soon see, to use the pagan tradition for his Ecclesiastical History—Eusebius knew that the Christians were a nation, and a victorious nation at that; and that their history could not be told except within the framework of the Church in which they lived. Furthermore, he was well aware that the Christian nation was what it was by virtue of its being both the oldest and the newest nation of the world. Its origins were twofold: coeval with the creation of the world and yet coeval with the birth of the Roman Empire under Augustus. True, this nation had no unique series of leaders to be compared with the succession of monarchs of other states. But the succession of the bishops in the apostolic sees represented the continuity of the legitimate heirs of Christ; whereas the preservation of the purity of the original teaching of the Apostles gave internal unity to the Church. Apostolic succession and doctrinal orthodoxy were the pillars of the new Christian nation; its enemies the persecutors and the heretics. Thus ecclesiastical history replaced the battles of ordinary political history by the trials inherent in resistance to persecution and heresy.

It is obvious that in developing this conception Eusebius had before him the Old Testament, Flavius Josephus, and the Acts of the Apostles. Each of these contributed something: the struggle against the persecutors had its precedents in the Books of Maccabees if not elsewhere; the idea of a holy nation was both in the Bible and in Josephus (and had been developed by earlier apologists); the spreading of Christianity had its classic document in the Acts of the Apostles. But in each case the differences were more marked than the similarities. In fact one of the important factors of Christian historiography is that there was no continuation to the Acts of the Apostles. They remained a document of the heroic age of Christianity, to be put together with the Gospels. More than two hundred years later Eusebius made a new start on a completely different basis: he was not primarily concerned with the spread of Christianity by propaganda and miracle, but with its survival of persecution and heresy from which it was to emerge victorious. The very fact that heresy in the Christian sense is absent from the Bible and from Josephus and plays as yet only a very small part in the Acts of the Apostles indicates the novelty of his approach. There was, however, one kind of account in pagan historiography that could help Eusebius considerably. That was the history of philosophical schools—such as we find it in Diogenes Laertius. To begin with, the idea of "succession," διαδοχή, was equally important in philosophical schools and in Eusebius' notion of Christianity. The bishops were the *diadochoi* of the Apostles, just as the *scholarchai* were the *diadochoi* of Plato, Zeno, and Epicurus. Second, like any philosophical school Christianity had its orthodoxy and its deviationists. Third, historians of philosophy in Greece used antiquarian methods and quoted documents much more frequently and thoroughly than their colleagues, the political historians. A glance at Diogenes Laertius is enough to show how pleased he is to produce original evidence for both the doctrine and the external vicissitudes of the philosophical schools he examines. Eusebius recognised the importance of documents for his History. As I said, direct original evidence was essential to establish the rightful claims of orthodoxy against external persecutors and internal dissidents. Here again we can be certain that Jewish influences were not without importance for Eusebius. The idea of scholarly succession is fundamental to rabbinic thought, which had developed in its turn under the impact of Greek theory. Moreover, Flavius Josephus had produced ample documents whenever he considered it necessary to prove Jewish rights; and documents were of course a conspicuous feature of the Books of Maccabees. But on the whole it was Hellenistic scholarship that Eusebius drew upon to shape the new model of ecclesiastical history. In this he was faithful to the Hellenistic tradition of his teachers and to his own programme in the *Praeparatio evangelica*.

The immense authority which Eusebius gained was well deserved. He had continuators but no rivals. The translation of his Ecclesiastical History into Latin by Rufinus was the starting point for ecclesiastical writing in the West. In the simplicity of its structure and in the matter of its documentation the Ecclesiastical History of Eusebius was one of the most authoritative prototypes ever created by ancient thought: indeed it was the last model elaborated by ancient historians for the benefit of later generations—if we except the Life of Antony by Athanasius, which became a model for later hagiography.

The simplicity of Eusebius' method was formidable but perhaps also deceptive. It was especially deceptive if applied to the post-Constantinian age, when the Church was no longer isolated by persecution. Eusebius' History of the Church ideally reflected the moment in which the Church had emerged victorious under Constantine—a separate body within the Roman Empire. With all his gifts Eusebius could not shape his historiography in such a way as to envisage situations in which it would be impossible to separate what belonged to Caesar from what belonged to Christ. There was a very real duality in Eusebius' notion of ecclesiastical history which was bound to become apparent as soon as the Christians were safely in command of the Roman state. On the one hand ecclesiastical history was the history of the

Christian nation now emerging as the ruling class of the Roman Empire. On the other hand it was the history of a divine institution not contaminated by political problems. As the history of the new ruling class of the Roman Empire ecclesiastical history had to include military and political events. But as a history of divine institutions ecclesiastical history was restricted to Church events. This duality has remained a major problem for all the ecclesiastical historians since Eusebius: no ecclesiastical historian has ever been able to concentrate exclusively on ecclesiastical affairs. Even the immediate continuators of Eusebius were compelled to take cognizance of some of those difficulties which are inevitably connected with the very notion of a divine Church: how to deal with this divine institution's very earthly relations with other institutions in terms of power, violence, and even territorial claims. A Church in power can hardly separate itself from the State in which it exercises its power. Furthermore, wherever Church and State tend to coalesce, it is difficult to separate heresy from political rebellion, dogmatic differences from court factions. How would the continuators of Eusebius deal with the politics of the emperors, the political intrigues of the bishops?

If we had the Christian History which the priest Philip of Side wrote about 430, we would know more about the difficulties of shaping an ecclesiastical history and about the significance of the predominance of the Eusebian model. It is evident that Philip of Side tried to go his own way and to avoid imitating Eusebius. His Christian History started with the origins of the world and included a great deal of natural science and mathematics, not to speak of geography. He apparently tried to provide a Christian encyclopaedia in the form of history. He was soon forgotten. The real continuators of Eusebius always included a certain amount of political history in their works. Quite typically they subdivided their histories according to the periods marked, not by bishops or metropolitans, but by Roman emperors.

None of the ecclesiastical historians of Late Antiquity ever claimed to have rendered political history superfluous. More or less clearly they presupposed the existence of other types of history. More particularly they recognised the existence of political history. The point is of great practical importance because it means that the rise of ecclesiastical history did not entail an interruption in the writing of ordinary political history. True, in the fourth and fifth centuries political history was mainly left in the hands of pagans, such as Ammianus Marcellinus, Nicomachus Flavianus, and Zosimus. But the fact that, according to Eusebius, Thucydides described the wickedness of the human race was no discouragement from reading Thucydides. The door was kept open for a Christian political historian like Procopius, who in the sixth century acknowledged Herodotus and Thucydides as his masters.

If Eusebius had no rival, none of his successors was so authoritative or persuasive as to exclude rivals. Just as Thucydides was continued by at least three historians, Eusebius had at least four successors (apart from his translator Rufinus), each starting from where he left off. Three of these are preserved and well known. Socrates dealt with the period from 303 to 439, Sozomenus from 303 to 421, Theodoretus from 303 to 428. Before them there had been Gelasius, Bishop of Caesarea between circa 365 and 400. The recovery of his lost work is one of the impressive achievements of patristic studies of this century. Gelasius undoubtedly continued Eusebius' Ecclesiastical History. Rufinus seems to have translated at least part of Gelasius of Caesarea when he added Books X and XI to his translation of Eusebius into Latin.

Socrates and Sozomenus were lawyers living in Constantinople; they were close to the imperial court. Socrates was very concerned with doctrinal differences within the Church. He treats them with the urbanity of a man who would rather do without them, though he has some sympathy with the Novatiani. Sozomenus, who makes large use of Socrates, is far more worldly than his mentor. He accepts the fact that by now Christianity is a state affair: in dedicating his work to Theodosius II he invites him to revise and censor what he has written. It is an open question whether Theodosius II exercised his censorship on Sozomenus.

Theodoretus takes us outside the capital. He was a provincial who had been deeply involved in the doctrinal controversies. He maintains an ominous silence on the Nestorian dispute of which he was one of the protagonists, but is otherwise outspoken, even brutal, in his partisan judgements. He warns the emperors that if they fail in their duty to orthodoxy they may be punished by God on the battlefield. However unpleasant Theodoretus may be at times, his is a very genuine voice. Nor can we separate his ecclesiastical history from his book on heresies and his profoundly pious and credulous account of the Syrian monks he had known, the *Historia Religiosa*.

The contemporaries themselves were aware that Gelasius of Caesarea, Socrates, Sozomenus, and Theodoretus were partial witnesses to the truth. About 475 Gelasius of Cyzicus tried to write a history of the ecclesiastical events of the East under Constantine (mainly about the Council of Nicaea) by combining Eusebius, Gelasius of Caesarea, Rufinus, Socrates, and Theodoretus and adding original documents. In the sixth century Theodorus Lector conceived the idea of conflating Socrates, Sozomenus, and Theodoretus in a *Historia Tripartita*, and this idea so pleased Cassiodorus that he had the work of Theodorus Lector partly translated and partly imitated in the *Historia Tripartita* in which Epiphanius was his collaborator. If we had the whole of the history of Philostorgius—which is preserved only in excerpts—we could see more clearly where these orthodox continuators of Eusebius went wrong. An Arian of the Eunomian variety, Philostorgius was their contemporary and wrote almost at the same time and on the same subject: his Ecclesiastical History started with the origins of the Arian controversy and went as far as A.D. 425. Being an Arian, Philostorgius was not complacent about the state of affairs in the Roman Empire. He adopted clear apocalyptic tones and liked to believe that the disaster of Adrianopolis in 378 was not unconnected with the persecution of the Arians. He saw the importance of the sack of Rome in 410, which is not mentioned by Theodoretus and only perfunctorily noticed by Socrates (VII, 10). The relatively more thoughtful remarks on the subject by Sozomenus (IX, 9–10) may well be due (as in other cases) to the influence of Philostorgius. It is indeed remarkable how loyal the three orthodox ecclesiastical historians remained to the Empire and how comparatively uninterested in what was happening outside it. Nothing is more instructive for their outlook than to see how they deal with the Christians outside the Empire. They devote little space to them, and almost invariably merely in order to discuss some specific measure of the Roman emperors. This is of course in keeping with the general trend of Christian propaganda, which was not very interested in the conversion of pagans outside the Empire.

III

After Justinian it became impossible in the West and difficult in the East to think historically in terms of a Universal Church. With the loss of the West to the Empire the oecumenical horizon of the Eusebian history was difficult to maintain. Christianity was no longer one nation, even as a fiction. Even in the East too much of it was outside the sphere controlled by the emperors of Constantinople. Moreover, Church events were becoming identical with state events; the great public controversies about heresy were being replaced by court intrigues. More than that—after the sixth century the East seems to have lost interest in oecumenical history altogether. Ecclesiastical history here followed in the wake of the general decline of historiography. The age of Procopius and Agathias is also the last great age of ecclesiastical historiography in the East. As far as I know, the monophysite John of Ephesus, who wrote in Syria about 585, and Euagrius Scholasticus, who ended his history after 594, are the last ecclesiastical historians who can claim direct descent from Eusebius. The Byzantine historian Nicephorus Callistus, who tried to revive ecclesiastical history about 1320—clearly under the impact of the new connections with the West—regretted that Euagrius had had no successor. Thus the gap was openly acknowledged in the East. In the West, as far as I can judge, the situation was more complex. Historiography in general was more vital, and ecclesiastical historiography had a share in this vitality. True, the first impression is that there was no place for a separate ecclesiastical historiography in the Middle Ages. Men thought in terms of fall and redemption: they divided the history of the world into three stages—*ante legem, sub lege, sub gratia*—and did not know of any clear distinction between Church and State. Even the notion of *duae civitates* was reinterpreted by Otto of Freising (about 1145) in the sense that from the times of Theodosius I to his own times one *civitas permixta* was the substance of history: "a temporis Theodosii senioris usque ad tempus nostrum non iam de duabus civitatibus, immo de una pene, id est ecclesia, sed permixta, historiam texuisse" (*M. G. H., Scriptores* t. XX, Hannover, 1868, 118–301). Otto had learned more from Orosius than from Augustine. I am not surprised that modern historians of ecclesiastical historiography jump from the *Historia Tripartita* by Cassiodorus to the Magdeburg *Centuriae* (1559). This is in keeping with the distrust of the Western Church for the philo-Arian Eusebius which is eloquently expressed in the *Decretum Gelasianum* (*P. L.* 59, col. 161) and which was reiterated by the great Spanish theologian Melchor Cano in the eleventh book of his *De Locis theologicis,* written a few years before the first *Centuriae.* Yet the fact remains that books written between the sixth and the fourteenth centuries received (more often by their authors than by their copyists) the title of Ecclesiastical History, and it would be very dangerous to assume that men like the Venerable Bede, Hugo of Fleury, Ordericus Vitalis, or Adam of Bremen did not know what they were doing when they entitled their works. Ordericus Vitalis regarded himself as belonging to a series of *scriptores ecclesiastici* which includes Eusebius, Orosius, Cassiodorus, and Paulus Diaconus (the last as the author of a history of the Bishopric of Metz). He modestly admitted that being a monk confined to his cloister he could not attempt to write the other kind of history which is concerned with the affairs of Alexandria, Greece, and Rome—the history which Dares Phrygius and Pompeius Trogus wrote. Not so precisely, but very eloquently, Adam of Bremen declared that as a son of the Church of Bremen and Hamburg he was obliged to tell the history of the Fathers of his Church. Also John of Salisbury, in what was a *Historia pontificalis* if not a *Historia ecclesiastica,* traced his ancestry to Luke, Eusebius, Cassiodorus, Orosius, Isidorus, and Bede. In the Middle Ages ecclesiastical historians did exist, they had an idea of their ancestry, and what matters to us is to see how they behaved in relation to the type of history which Eusebius had created.

First of all, the Eusebian type of history remained well known to the readers of the West, and there was at least one attempt to revive it. Eusebius, in Rufinus' translation, was read throughout the Middle Ages. He was of course known to Gregory of Tours, Bede, Isidorus, and there were some eloquent references to his name in Augustine. The very numerous manuscripts of Rufinus show how much he had been read at least since the ninth century. Even without Rufinus mediaeval clerics would have been reminded of the Eusebian type of history by the popular *Historia Tripartita* of Cassiodorus-Epiphanius, 137 manuscripts of which were inspected by its most recent editor. Sozomenus, in so far as he was utilised by the *Historia Tripartita*, was severely criticised by Gregory the Great at the end of the sixth century, and this criticism was still remembered by Anastasius Bibliothecarius in the ninth century. It was Anastasius who with Johannes Diaconus conceived the idea of reviving the Eusebian type of universal ecclesiastical history after 870. The experiences of the eighth Oecumenical Council of Constantinople, in which Anastasius had taken part as an expert in Greek language and theology, persuaded him that it was indispensable for the Church of Rome to be informed of past ecclesiastical events. He therefore agreed to provide the translation of the Greek authorities upon which Johannes Diaconus was to build a new ecclesiastical history of the Eusebian type—avoiding, however, the doctrinal errors for which Gregory the Great had criticised Sozomenus (or Epiphanius). Anastasius speaks of a history which would include all the important events since the birth of Christ—"ut quae ab ipso Christi adventu in Ecclesia gesta sunt et textu ecclesiasticae historiae non iudicantur indigna" (*P. G.* 108, col. 1190). He was clearly thinking of a Eusebian kind of history. But Johannes Diaconus never found the time or the inspiration to write the history planned by Anastasius: the Eusebian history was well remembered, but not revived.

The right conclusion would appear to be that the Eusebian form of ecclesiastical historiography was abandoned in the West not because of ignorance but because of the instinctive search for something more in accordance with contemporary needs—that is, with the creation of national states and local units. At the same time, the abandonment was not complete because each writer kept faith with the Eusebian premises of the existence of a Universal Church and of the necessity for documentary evidence.

Naturally enough the prevailing pattern of mediaeval ecclesiastical history is that which emphasises local events of a particular see or monastery. The writers take Christianity for granted and concentrate on the individual corporation in conformity with the prevailing trend of social life. The continuity of the institution is represented by the succession of bishops or abbots, the contents of the history are a mixture of biography and local chronicle. What happened to the bishop or abbot is what happened to the institution; and what he did is what the church or monastery did—though chroniclers are human enough to register internal squabbles. Hence the sincerity and freshness of their accounts. It is difficult to forget that king of the Danes who, according to Adam of Bremen, "noted attentively and remembered everything the archbishop drew from the Scriptures, with the exception that he could not be convinced about gluttony and women, which vices are inborn with that people. As to everything else, the king was obedient and yielding to the prelate" (3, 21, transl. F. J. Tschan). Unlike their ancient and their modern colleagues mediaeval ecclesiastical historians could smile. And Flodoardus, the historian of the *Ecclesia Remensis*, reminds us how hard it was to write when there was so little defence against bitter winter and books were in short supply (Prologue). But at no time between the seventh and the fifteenth centuries were the ecclesiastical historians content to be the chroniclers of their own particular institution. The need to go beyond it, to reach the large body of the Christian community, is apparent everywhere. The notion of the Church as the *Ecclesia Christi* is too strong in every historian to allow him to be satisfied with remaining the historian of the Bishopric of Metz or of Rheims or of the Monastery of Saint-Gall. These historians were well aware that their particular institution was only a fragment of Christianity and that in the notion of Christianity there was never any sharp distinction between political and religious affairs. Again and again we observe in mediaeval ecclesiastical historians of any century the transition from local ecclesiastical history to general ecclesiastical history, and even more frequently the transition from Church history to mundane history. Ordericus Vitalis in the early twelfth century starts as a historian of his own monastery of Saint-Évroul in Normandy and ends as a general historian of the Normans, which in the circumstances means a historian of Byzantines, Crusaders, Saracens— and yet he calls his work *Ecclesiastica historia*. Even more emphatically his contemporary Hugo of Fleury expands his *Ecclesiastica his-*

toria into a *Chronica mundi*, a *Weltchronik*. A closer analysis of the two redactions of his *Ecclesiastica historia* would show Hugo's struggle to shape his history in a satisfactory manner: it would also show what he learned from Anastasius Bibliothecarius, whom he discovered after having completed the first redaction. But even those ecclesiastical chronicles which, more modestly, confined themselves to their own institution were apt to transcend the ecclesiastical as well as the geographical limits of their subject. Some books, such as Bede's *Ecclesiastical History of the English Nation*, tell the history of the conversion of one region to Christianity, and much more besides; others, like the Ecclesiastical History of Hamburg by Adam of Bremen in the eleventh century, tell the history of the spreading of Christianity among the Northern nations as a result of the missionary activity of one bishopric: part of his Church history is a splendid geographical excursus worthy of Herodotus. In the late Middle Ages, especially in England and in Italy, where papal authority was stronger, the succession of the Bishops of Rome was emphasised as the backbone of universal history: this is apparent, for instance, in the Pontifical History of John of Salisbury and later in the *Historia ecclesiastica nova* of Tolomeo da Lucca (Bartolomeo Fiadoni), who both took the history of the popes as the guiding thread. Social and political conditions in the Middle Ages naturally favoured the writing of chronicles of individual institutions. But the notion of the Universal Church informed the telling of local events. Indeed the notion of a Universal Church implies a paradox. Being universal, Church history tended to embrace all the events of mankind and was therefore permanently in danger of losing its distinctive character.

The Eusebian form of ecclesiastical history was brought back in full force by the Reformation, just as the Thucydidean form of political history was brought back by Italian political life in the age of humanism. The example of Eusebius acted far more directly than the example of Thucydides. In 1519 Luther made himself familiar with Eusebius in Rufinus' translation. In 1530 Caspar Hedio published the *Chronica der alten christlichen Kirchen aus Eusebius und der Tripartita*. Flacius Illyricus and his team of centuriators knew their Eusebius by heart, of course—and the same can be said of all the ecclesiastical historians who worked after them, be it in the Protestant or in the Catholic camp. What both Protestants and Catholics wanted to prove was that they had the authority of the first centuries of the Church on their side. Consequently the ecclesiastical history that the religious controversies of the sixteenth century demanded was a history of the Universal Church—not a history of special churches. Eusebius was the model of a universal historian of the Church, his concern with the apostolic sees was still helpful, and his collection of documents and quotations was the natural starting point for further erudite research.

In many ways Flacius Illyricus went beyond his Eusebian model. The standards of precise documentation were far more severe in the sixteenth than in the fourth century. Above all the questions asked by the new controversialists within the framework of the history of the Universal Church were different from those of Eusebius. Eusebius dealt with heresies, but he had no suspicion that the very course of events of the first Christian centuries could be disputed and that there might be more than one interpretation of basic events. The position of St. Peter, the development of ecclesiastical hierarchy, the origin and development of at least certain sacraments were not a matter of controversy to him. They were, needless to say, at the centre of attention both by Flacius Illyricus and by Cesare Baronio, who, after attempts by others, at last produced the Catholic answer to the Protestant ecclesiastical historiography. What characterises the new historiography of the Reformation and Counter-Reformation is the search for the true image of Early Christianity to be opposed to the false one of the rivals— whereas Eusebius wanted to show how Christianity had emerged triumphant from persecution. The idea of a Christian nation, which had been central to Eusebius, therefore became devoid of any reality for Flacius, Baronio, and their followers. They were concerned not so much with the Christians as with Christian institutions and doctrines.

Yet there can be no doubt that in their efforts to establish the true development of Early Christianity the ancient historians of Eusebius' school were constantly in their minds. The immense labour of Scaliger on Eusebius' chronology, and Valesius' commentary on Eusebius and the other ancient ecclesiastical historians, are among the results of this study. When Casaubon and Salmasius wanted to attack Baronio's reliability as a historian, they turned freely to the early Church historians. In the Prolegomena to his *Exercitationes XVI ad Cardinalis Baronii Prolegomena in Annales* (1614) Casaubon eloquently emphasises the importance of Eusebius and his school in comparison with the later decline of ecclesiastical history. As long as the notion of a Universal Church was not in dispute, Eusebius remained the source of inspiration for ecclesiastical historians. The enormous, almost pathological, output of ecclesiastical history in the seventeenth and eighteenth centuries becomes more and more involved in discussions of details, and more and more diversified in theological outlook, but it never repudiates the basic notion that a Universal Church exists beyond the individual Christian communities. Even the revolutionary Gottfried Arnold, who sees the real Church outside every existing denomination, does not yet doubt that the true *ecclesia* exists somewhere.

The history of the Church was bound to change its character when the existence of an invisible, Universal Church was no longer taken for granted—and therefore the praeludium in heaven with which Eusebius had prefaced his history on earth became at least controversial, if not superfluous or ridiculous. It is of course impossible to indicate the exact moment in which the history of the Church began to be studied as the history of a human community instead of a divine institution. Some may think that the turning point is represented by the *Institutionum historiae ecclesiasticae* of Johann Lorenz von Mosheim which appeared in 1755, others may put the burden on Hegel's pupil Ferdinand Christian Baur, others again may well think that Max Weber with his Sociology of Religions was the first to put the Christian Church on a level with any other religious society—or perhaps with any other human society. If I had to produce my own candidate, I would go back to the first half of the eighteenth century and name Pietro Giannone, who meditated deeply on the relation between ecclesiastical and political history and about 1742 wrote in prison a sketch of the history of ecclesiastical history which could be published only in 1859 (*Istoria del Pontificato di Gregorio Magno* in *Opere* di Pietro Giannone, ed. Bertelli-Ricuperati, Naples, 1971, 964). The truth is of course that the historians of the Church are still divided on the fundamental issue of the divine origin of the Church. The number of

professional historians who take the Church as a divine institution—
and can therefore be considered the followers of Eusebius—increased
rather than decreased in the years after the First World War. On the
other hand the historians who study the history of the Church as that
of a human institution have consolidated their methods. They have
been helped by the general adoption in historiography of those standards of erudite research which seemed at one time to have been confined to ecclesiastical historians and controversialists. We sometimes
forget that Eduard Meyer was, at least in Germany, the first nontheo-
logian to write a scholarly history of the origins of Christianity, and
this happened only in 1921. It is the dispute between those who believe
in the supernatural character of the Church and those who do not believe in it which is really behind the rather tedious dissertations on the
"Begriff der Kirche bei den Kirchenhistorikern" and the "Gegenstand
der Kirchengeschichte." Those who accept the notion of the Church as
a divine institution which is different from the other institutions have
to face the difficulty that Church history reveals only too obviously a
continuous mixture of political and religious aspects: hence the distinction frequently made by Church historians of the last two centuries
between internal and external history of the Church, where internal
means (more or less) religious and external means (more or less) political. By contrast the historians of the Church as a worldly institution
have to reckon with the difficulty of describing without the help of a
belief what has existed through the help of a belief. As far as I can see,
no reconciliation is possible between these two ways of seeing the history of the Church; though love for truth, respect for evidence, and
care for details can do much, and have done much, to help mutual understanding and tolerance, even collaboration, of believers and
unbelievers.

At the beginning of this imposing movement of research and controversy there remains Eusebius of Caesarea. In 1834 Ferdinand Christian Baur wrote in Tübingen a comparison between Eusebius and Herodotus: *Comparatur Eusebius Caesarensis historiae ecclesiasticae
parens cum parente historiarum Herodoto Halicarnassensi*. We can accept this comparison and meditate on his remark that both Herodotus
and Eusebius wrote under the inspiration of a newly established
freedom.

Conclusion

At the beginning of these six lectures I said that I conceived them as the first part of a trilogy. I want to explore in future courses the conflict between the Greek and the Jewish vision of the world where I am competent to study it, that is, in the Hellenistic period; and I want to face certain aspects of modern historical research. I shall therefore postpone my general conclusion, which implies questions about the nature, function, limits, and methods of historical research. But I may perhaps conclude this first series of lectures with a few remarks confined within the limits of my strictly personal experience.

When I was young I was told by my teachers that Herodotus invented history, and Thucydides perfected the invention. The later ancient historians corrupted what Thucydides had perfected. Thucydides did not come into his own again until Machiavelli and Guicciardini revived the ancient conception of political history. True, the Christian idea of Providence was a potential contribution to a better historiography. But the Middle Ages did not produce real historians. The potentialities of the providential conception of history were not realised until the eighteenth century, when the Heavenly City of St. Augustine was secularised into the Heavenly City of Voltaire. The next step was the Romantic idea of History, which combined Thucydides with Voltaire. Some of my teachers preferred Ranke as the model historian, others preferred Droysen or even Dilthey. But the scheme was fundamentally the same. It is to be found in Croce and (partly by implication) in Meinecke. It was presented to the American public as late as 1949 by a very authoritative representative of German historical thought, Hajo Holborn, in an article on Greek and Modern Concepts of History in the *Journal of the History of Ideas*.

Like every student of ancient history of my generation I had to think again about the most elementary principles of my own subject. Slowly, and yet imperfectly, I have formed a much more complex picture of the relation between ancient historical thought and modern historical thought. Some of the elements of the picture—certainly not all of them, probably not even the most important—I have tried to present in these lectures.

Antiquity did not create one type of history only. It created many types. Who wants to understand what historiography is about has to come to terms with this plurality of types. I hope to have shown that the disappearance of the powerful Hebrew historiography after the Maccabees is a major problem in the history of ideas. I hope also to have shown that we must not concede to Thucydides that he really replaced Herodotus. A Herodotean tradition of historiography did survive, and very useful it was to prevent history from becoming an exclusive instrument of political analysis. One is entitled to be suspicious even of great scholars like Werner Jaeger when they cannot include Herodotus in their idea of paideia. It also became obvious that the reception of Greek historiography in Rome was more than mere transmission of an alien product. The manner of this reception determined for good or ill the future of European historiography. European national history and historiographical classicism derived from it. But at least one Roman historian had the spiritual energy to examine his own place in his own time without being unduly intimidated by the Greeks. This historian, Tacitus, was one of the masters of modern political thought from the Counter-Reformation to the early nineteenth century. The very extent of his influence among nonhistorians is significant.

Tacitus was from the start an ambiguous writer. There was no such initial ambiguity in Eusebius. His Ecclesiastical History was a formidable assertion of independence from the State and of intolerance towards the unbeliever and the heretic. This attitude has remained the source of the vitality of ecclesiastical history down to the nineteenth century.

Equally important seems to me the role played by the antiquarians in historical thought. In Antiquity and in the Renaissance historians were seldom able to reach out to the remote past and only seldom did they handle original evidence or care for cultural history. It was left to the antiquarians to organise the study of cultural history and to explore the remains of the more remote past. It is difficult to separate antiquarianism from biographical research. Biography, which first appeared in the fifth century and flourished in Hellenistic and Roman times, was always something of a mixed genre: it still is. But nobody can deny its vitality.

The influence of the antiquarians is also apparent in ecclesiastical history. The ability with which ecclesiastical historians assimilated the methods of antiquarian research contributed to their strength. The political historians absorbed the methods and aims of the antiquarians only later and more slowly.

Now in one sense the struggle between antiquarians and historians is over. The antiquarians are no longer needed as the custodians of cultural history and of archaelogical remains: they are therefore disappearing. But there is another aspect of antiquarian work which is not obsolete. The antiquarians liked systematic handbooks and static descriptions. Though unable to grasp the changes, they were certainly able to trace the connections. Pure historians know what changes are, but are less good at discovering what is structural. As long as historians cannot produce a remedy for this deficiency, sociology will remain the refurbished form of antiquarianism which our age requires.

Two questions are in my mind just as they are, I am sure, in your minds. One is whether sociology and history can ultimately remain separate disciplines. The other is whether an ecclesiastical history has the right to exist in the present conditions of historical research.

Let me remind you by way of conclusion that I have purposely avoided discussing the more profound reasons why the Greek and Roman methods of history writing were revived in the Renaissance. Antiquity thought man to be mortal—nature to be immortal. Christianity made the individual immortal but was prepared to accept the end of nature as an event to be expected in the foreseeable future. Machiavelli, Guicciardini, Commynes, Mariana, Hayward no doubt believed in individual immortality and in the transience of nature, in so far as they remained members of the Christian society. But as historians they were concerned to bestow literary immortality on mortal beings and to provide useful information for a world which was expected to last. The separation of religion and politics is at the root of modern historiography. Paradoxically, Christian ideas penetrated into modern historical books only in the eighteenth and nineteenth centuries, when faith in Christianity was at its lowest. This was due to the attempt at giving one meaning to the historical process as a whole—from the origins of the world to the triumph of reason or to the advent of the classless society. When that happened, modern historical methods had already been shaped upon their ancient models. Modern philosophy of history—on a Christian basis—and modern historical methods—on a classical basis—have never quite agreed with each other. It would take another book—one which I should probably not be able to write—to disentangle the implications of this elementary fact.

An ancient historian must be particularly grateful if he is offered an opportunity to speak to the students of the humanities at large. Only by these contacts can he realise how narrow his normal outlook is, how much more intelligent the students of modern history are.

The Sather Classical Lectures are a famous occasion for these wider encounters, so famous that it has been observed that a man makes his reputation by being invited to deliver them and loses his reputation by delivering them.

Whatever may be the outcome in my case, I am grateful for the encounters.

Index of Names